Thinking Skills and
Problem-Solving
An Inclusive Approach

Thinking Skills and Problem-Solving

An Inclusive Approach

A Practical Guide for Teachers in Primary Schools

**Belle Wallace, June Maker, Diana Cave
and Simon Chandler**

David Fulton Publishers

in association with
The National Association for Able Children in Education

David Fulton Publishers
2 Park Square, Milton Park, Abingdon, Oxon OX14 4RN

270 Madison Avenue, New York, NY 10016

First published in Great Britain in 2004 by David Fulton Publishers
Transferred to digital printing

David Fulton Publishers is an imprint of the Taylor & Francis Group, an informa business

British Library Cataloguing in Publication Data
A catalogue record for this book is available from the British Library.

ISBN 1 84312 107 7

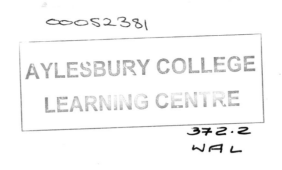
Typeset by FiSH Books, London

Contents

Notes on Contributors

Belle Wallace is known internationally for her work with very able children, and also for her work as a researcher and developer of a problem-solving and thinking skills base for curriculum development. She maintains that the performance levels of all pupils can be raised when they are systematically taught a range of problem-solving and thinking skills, and she has developed curricula internationally for disadvantaged learners. She is particularly keen to infuse problem-solving and thinking skills across the curriculum in all areas of human abilities. Since its inception in 1982, she has been editor of the journal *Gifted Education International*. She has published widely, served on the Executive Board of the World Council for Gifted and Talented Children (WCGTC), and is currently President of the National Association for Able Children in Education, UK (NACE). Her particular interest is in working with teachers to develop their expertise in the teaching of problem-solving and thinking skills across the National Curriculum. She has written and edited a series of practical classroom-based texts for the Teaching of Thinking Skills at Early Years, Primary and Middle Years (London: David Fulton Publishers, in association with NACE).

C. June Maker's work is known internationally in the field of performance-based assessment of problem-solving in multiple domains and curricula designed to enhance the strengths and talents of all students. She is principal investigator of the DISCOVER Projects, a series of research and development projects funded by governmental agencies such as the Javits Gifted and Talented Education Programme and the Office of Bilingual Education and Minority Language Affairs. DISCOVER Projects also have a strong emphasis on arts integration, a constructivist philosophy, and the development of students' sense of self-esteem. Her current research centres on finding and developing the talents of underserved groups such as Native American, Hispanic American, African American and Asian American and students with disabilities. June is Professor of Special Education at the University of Arizona, Tucson, USA, where she co-ordinates graduate degrees at specialist and doctoral levels. She has served on the Board of NAGC (USA), is consultant to numerous state districts and departments both nationally and internationally, and has participated at conferences worldwide. Her publications include topics such as gifted handicapped, gifted minority students, creativity and problem-solving and alternative modes of assessement.

Diana Cave began her teaching career in middle schools in Warwickshire and for the past 13 years has taught in The National School, Grantham, Lincolnshire. During this time she has held a number of consecutive posts with special responsibility, namely: Year 3 Team Leader coordinating work across the year and liaising with local infant schools; Year 6 Team Leader; Assessment Coordinator and Curriculum Coordinator. She has consequently acquired a unique range of experience across both subject areas and year groups. She was one of the major contributors to *Teaching Thinking Skills Across the Primary Curriculum: A practical approach for all abilities* and to *Using History to Develop Thinking Skills* (both London: David Fulton Publishers, in association with NACE).

Simon Chandler has taught in a wide range of primary schools – small, large, urban, rural – and has also taught in a special school for children with Moderate Learning Difficulties. He is currently head teacher of a school that has undergone rapid improvement over the past few years. Simon is determined to provide the best quality education for children in his school and is constantly looking for new and effective ways to improve provision, while reducing teachers' workloads. TASC (Thinking Actively in a Social Context), along with other strategies, has been pivotal in bringing about the positive changes in the school and is recognised locally as being effective and motivational for pupils.

Acknowledgements

Very little is achieved without teamwork and there are always so many 'behind the scenes' contributors to a book such as this. In particular, Belle and June would like to thank the teachers, students and children who have helped with the action research that underpins the work of this book, and who have undertaken to trial, refine and reflect on the principles and practice we now share with our colleagues around the world.

We would particularly like to thank Diana Cave who, over a number of years, has provided leadership and encouragement to her colleagues enabling them to work in depth to trial the TASC (Thinking Actively in a Social Context) Problem-solving Model, and also the DISCOVER (Discovering Intellectual Strengths and Capabilities while Observing Varied Ethnic Responses) Model. She unfailingly brings a deep understanding and commitment to the principles of good practice, and always 'walks the tenth mile' to achieve her aims of providing an enabling curriculum for all children.

Thanks, too, to Simon Chandler who has been eager to negotiate with his staff their involvement in professional debate and whole-school development revolving around the TASC Problem-solving Framework, and who ventured to plan and carry out a 'multiple abilities week' in which teachers and children explored their strengths across a range of activities. The teachers were willing to take risks and trial a range of problem-solving activities, and they were willing to spend time in discussion and reflection so that the activities could be refined.

We give our thanks to the following schools who are using the TASC Framework across the curriculum, and who have supplied the photographs and examples of children's work throughout the book.

The National CE Junior School, Grantham, Lincs.
John Gibbs (head teacher), Diana Cave, Jayne Lewis, Emily Featherstone, Susan Nadin, Victoria Wright, Richard Jefferies, Diane Ramsay, Jane Johns, Heather Banks, Wendy Britton, Nicola Haylock, Miriam Core, Mark Wesson, Elizabeth Woods, Mari Mander, Stephen Chamberlain, Teresa Thomas, Christine Ball. We would also like to include the Learning Support Assistants who provide such valuable day-to-day support, and who, during DISCOVER/TASC activities, are invaluable assistants especially for those children who need extra support: Christine Farmilo, Mavis Deptford, Lynda Kirton, Joanne Franklin, Gaynor Mckay, Kathryn Franklin, Amanda Young.

Claremont Primary School, Grantham, Lincs.
Simon Chandler (head teacher), Maxine Purvis, Ruth Devine, Becky Bason, Becky Williams, Gill Steeples, Sarah Mitchell, Jayne Allen, Ann Sanger; and the valued team of Learning Support Assistants: Elaine Green, Wendy Truman, Diane Found, Kim Shales, Tina Bell.

Little Gonerby CE Infants' School, Grantham, Lincs.
Elizabeth Wiggins (head teacher), Lesley Norton, Marguerite Tibbett, Veronica Phillips, Terry Beese, Amy Stancer, Denise Taylor; and the Learning Support Assistants: Rosemary Betts, Sue Kelly, Karen Rigby.

Gonerby Hill Foot CE Primary School, Grantham, Lincs.
Peter Riches (head teacher), Kay Sutherland, Marion Arch, Joan Baty, Rachel Bensley, Jenny Dalton, Duncan Jones, Lisa Radford, Nita Johnson, Tricia McLean, Denise Macey, Richard Tomlinson, Lin Wall; and the Learning Support Assistants: Sharon Liddiard, Pauline Jeffrey, Melita Copley, Karen Hannigan, Sue Wainwright, Gill Noon, Jackie McLoughlin, Sue Dowse, Rachel Clare.

St Mary's RC Primary School, Grantham, Lincs.
Linda Heaver (head teacher), Fran Moreton, Christine Duffy, Hannah Barnett, Clare Webster, Rachel Kirkby, Sudha Howell, Darren Price, Janice Corcoran; and the ancillary staff: Chris Leonard, Val Carter, L. Bint, Paddy Wilson, Judy Nagy, Sarah Williamson.

For Children, Parents and Teachers

Belle Wallace and June Maker have wanted to work together for a long time, and now, together with Diana Cave and Simon Chandler, have joyfully combined their work in this book. Both June and Belle have worked for a number of years internationally with many cultures in many different parts of the world. June has been engaged in developing problem-solving curricula and has focused on *types* of problems that learners should engage with across the full range of human abilities. Belle has focused on the *processes* of problem-solving, also working across the whole spectrum of human abilities.

We are committed to the belief that all children are born with potential, and that if parents and teachers actively engage with children in problem-solving activities, then children will learn lifelong skills and behaviours that will enable them to live their lives more effectively and with greater joy as they realise their capacities. We are also committed to the belief that developing the full range of children's potential enables every child to be successful, because every child has strengths she or he can celebrate; and through the celebration of what they *can* do well, they gain the courage to persevere with their weaknesses.

We also believe that there is celebration in the diversity of human beings: that differences are a source of pleasure as humane ideas and viewpoints are expressed and understood with genuine respect for others' strengths, beliefs and lifestyles. We often hear and talk about the 'global' community, and we need to develop our children's awareness of their global citizenship, their responsibilities and, as a consequence, their earned rights. We are all aware that the world around us is becoming increasingly complex and troubled; and our children will need both the courage and the skills to confront these problems if the world is ever to become a decent place for all to live.

So this book is dedicated to parents and teachers in the belief that committed adults are concerned to nurture the young in their care, and we have had the great privilege of working with teachers in creating curricular activities that develop a humanising and empowering education. We believe that this book is a celebration of what good teachers can do in the development of best classroom practice.

The first three chapters explore and justify what we mean by the development of a curriculum that teaches children to think more effectively. If we believe that education should nurture skills for lifelong learning, then this means that teachers (and also parents) need to be consciously aware of the ways they interact with children: the behaviours they are modelling, the language they are developing, the work habits they are inculcating, the values and beliefs they are encouraging, the pattern of responsibilities they are demonstrating. Life behaviour is learned and copied from adults, and children mirror what they see and experience.

Chapters 4 and 5 put the principles discussed in the first three chapters into practice in everyday classrooms. Many teachers have contributed to this, demonstrating the qualities they possess as gifted professionals, dedicated to the children in their care. Importantly, these chapters are written by teachers who are willingly sharing their best practice with their colleagues, so that all children can benefit.

Belle and June are privileged to have worked alongside them.

The Rich Spectrum of ○ ❶ ○○
Human Potential
Influences on the development of human abilities and capacities

> Every human being has the potential to manifest the finest mosaic of attributes in a dazzling complexity of difference and diversity. Yet so often, this human mosaic is dull and tarnished – only a hint of the incipient splendour remains. And yet, sometimes, we are inspired by the light radiated from an individual.
>
> (Belle Wallace)

This chapter outlines the key principles which maximise the development of children's learning. We examine the constituents that produce a rich learning environment in which children can develop their vital general learning capacities: intuition, memory, creativity, reasoning or logic, and metacognition which is the super-ordinate learning capacity.

The chapter also discusses the full range of human abilities together with the learning processes and competencies or outcomes which should inform a curriculum that aims to develop thinking and problem-solving.

Appendix 1 on pages 133–50 is arranged in three main parts:

● Appendix 1A provides practical teacher observational checklists outlining:

1A.i   general problem-solving abilities

and the core characteristics that are specific to each human ability:

1A.ii   core characteristics for Foundation Key Stage 1 (4- to 7-year-olds)

1A.iii core characteristics for Key Stage 2 (7- to 11-year-olds)

● Appendix 1B provides suggestions for practical activities that allow children to display these characteristics.

● Appendix 1C provides checklists for reflection on preferred activities across the full range of human abilities:

Checklist 1 provides a reflective checklist of preferred activities for children at the upper end of Key Stage 2. This supplements the experience of working across the full range of activities suggested in Appendix B.

Checklist 2 provides a reflective checklist of preferred activities for teachers who need to recognise fully the profile of their own abilities so that they have a clearer understanding of their own preferred learning and teaching modes.

Every child is born with huge potential for learning – potential for a wide range of human abilities to develop and manifest through rich human activity. Current neuro-biological research suggests that rich experiential play in the early years of brain development activates and establishes a complex network of connections which children need for later learning in physical, social, emotional and cognitive domains. Parents and teachers play a vital role in this development, interacting, extending experiences, acting as role-models, and providing examples and opportunities for practice.

There is a range of key principles that characterise the optimum development of children's potential. These principles constitute the essential factors that should combine to enrich the interaction between children and their parents, mentors or teachers. The principles are outlined below.

Key principles in maximising the development of children's learning

1. Within a rich environment of learning experiences, young learners use vital general learning capacities: intuition, memory, creativity, logical thinking, and metacognition. These capacities dynamically interact in the process of problem-solving.

2. Problem-solving should optimally take place using the full range of human abilities.

3. Through a developing network of learning processes, children need to acquire a range of competencies or outcomes.

4. Children should understand their problem-solving processes and should use these processes across a wide range of problem-solving activities.

We need now to analyse and break down the principles highlighted above and to look in depth at these interrelated components that bring about children's effective learning.

What constitutes a rich environment of learning experiences?

June Maker and Usanee Anuruthwong (in press) use the metaphor of a tree when discussing children's learning environments. They suggest that the growth of a tree responds to the amount of water available – too much rots the tree, while too little stunts its growth. Nevertheless, many trees adapt to their growth environments. Similarly, an 'over-rich' environment can flood a child with too many sensations and too much stimulation, denying the child's own essentially individual personality and her or his need for personal space and adequate rest. Conversely, an 'impoverished' environment denies the child rich experiential opportunities and development is stunted. These experiential opportunities are both *physical* in the sense of the actual surroundings and *dynamic* in the sense of the quality of human interaction.

We could think of optimal environmental influence as lying somewhere along the continuum shown in Mindmap 1.

Mindmap 1: The continuum of influential environmental factors

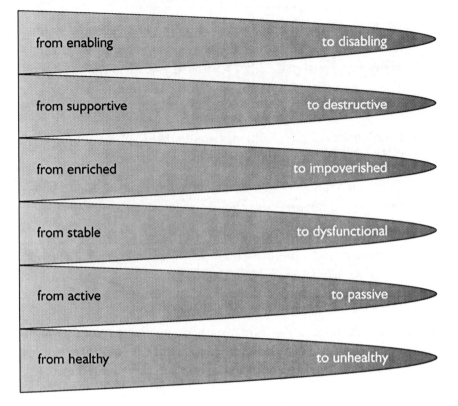

from enabling	to disabling
from supportive	to destructive
from enriched	to impoverished
from stable	to dysfunctional
from active	to passive
from healthy	to unhealthy

However, many children not only survive but triumph over potentially disabling environments, and usually there is at least one enabling factor – such as the child's own inner resilience, perception and determination, or an adult/mentor who supports and encourages.

REFLECT

● In what ways do the early years and primary classrooms foster an enabling environment for children?

● What can schools do to help parents understand children's need for rich experiences, quality time and interaction?

What do we mean by vital general learning capacities?

Recent theorists argue that 'intelligence' is the capacity for problem-solving, both with regard to everyday life problems, and also with regard to so-called 'academic' and 'practical' problems such as those that occur, for example, at all levels in maths and science or history and literature.

We call into action a number of capacities that are interdependent and interactive during the process of problem-solving. These are illustrated in Mindmap 2.

Mindmap 2: Vital general learning capacities

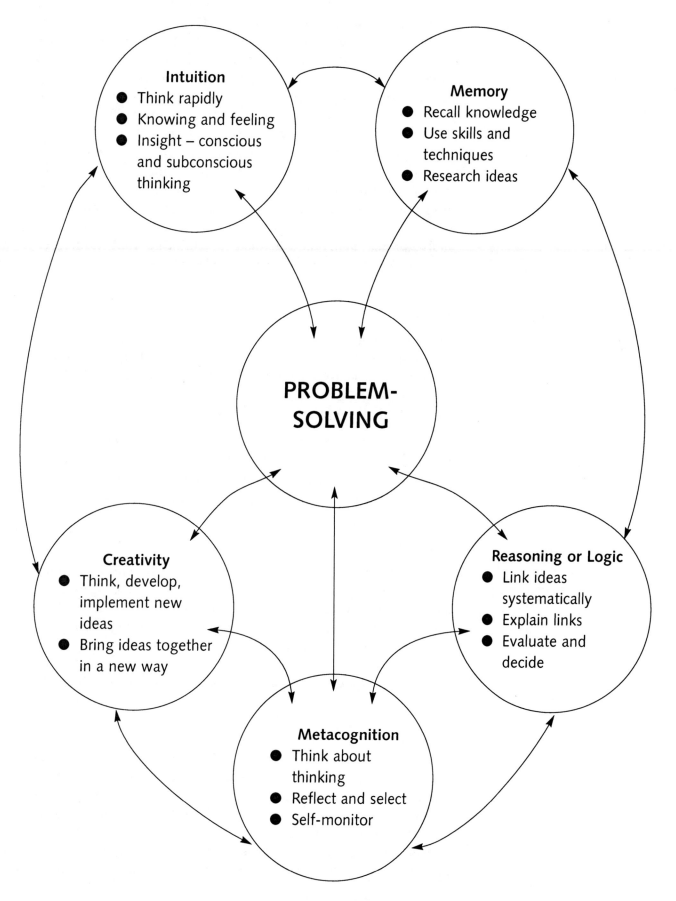

Intuition
- Think rapidly
- Knowing and feeling
- Insight – conscious and subconscious thinking

Memory
- Recall knowledge
- Use skills and techniques
- Research ideas

PROBLEM-SOLVING

Creativity
- Think, develop, implement new ideas
- Bring ideas together in a new way

Reasoning or Logic
- Link ideas systematically
- Explain links
- Evaluate and decide

Metacognition
- Think about thinking
- Reflect and select
- Self-monitor

Intuition

Intuition is the capacity to 'know something immediately'. The thinking is rapid, it may be logical and creative, and it combines rapid understanding and insight that uses elements of both subconscious and conscious thinking. Children have a great capacity for intuitive understanding – knowing and feeling before they develop language to express that understanding and feeling. We could refer to their intuitive understanding as their 'first language' and call the sounds and symbols they learn to express ideas their 'second language'. Many very able children process knowledge and information so rapidly that they have difficulty explaining the steps of their thinking when they are asked to 'write down the stages'. While many adults retain and use their capacity for intuitive thinking in diverse scenarios, sadly all too many adults distrust thinking that cannot be broken down into obviously connected logical steps.

Memory

Everyone needs a store of knowledge that is experiential or acquired through finding out about the world. Everyone also needs knowledge that is specific to a particular ability, for example wide language vocabulary, maths sequences, decoding and spelling, music notation and dance movement.

We use both experiential and ability-specific knowledge in the process of problem-solving. The child has tremendous memory capacity for learning new ability-specific knowledge and skills when the learning is embedded in real-life experiential contexts.

Creativity

Creativity is the general capacity to think of, develop, and implement new or appropriate ideas and solutions, or to bring unusual ideas together in a new way. The creative capacity can result in a personally creative idea or product, as happens often with young children, or in an idea or product that is universally 'new', as is the case with older, more experienced and mature learners. Creative thinking is an essential element in problem-solving.

Reasoning or Logic

Reasoning or logic is the capacity to link ideas in systematic steps that can be explained or justified. However, there are different modes of logic. For example, the logical steps needed to explain a solution to a maths problem are quite different from the logic needed to support an argument about a character in a story. Reasoning or logical thinking is used when evaluating ideas in problem-solving and also is a key element in critical thinking.

Metacognition

Metacognition involves problem-solving processes and thinking about thinking. This reflection allows for the selection of capacities that are relevant to problem-solving: when to use creative thinking, when to use logical thinking, when to use specific knowledge or skills, when to rely on intuition. Metacognition uses images, words and thoughts and constitutes the important overall 'monitor' of the use of human capacities.

- To what extent does the National Curriculum Framework allow for and encourage opportunities for children to develop and practise general learning capacities?

- How can teachers create space in their lesson planning so that children have opportunities to use and develop these learning capacities?

What do we mean by the full range of human abilities?

Humans have a wonderful range of at least ten human abilities – a wide spectrum of abilities that combine in different ways to solve problems, deal with challenges and create new ideas and products. We each have *all* the abilities but we have different profiles of strengths and preferred modes of working across the full range of these abilities. Also the opportunities presented to us either encourage or discourage the optimum development of these abilities.

Children need to be literate and numerate, and to have an understanding in science, but we would stress that all the human abilities are important. Below is a list of the full range of human abilities in the order that they are presented in the National Curriculum Framework and not according to our priority. An overview of them is provided in Mindmap 3 (pp. 14–15).

- **Social/Humanitarian abilities** comprise the understanding and skills we need to get along with other people. At the highest level of development we see people engaged in responsible and caring leadership, humanitarian projects and endeavours, and concern for human rights and responsibilities. The development of Social, Emotional and Spiritual abilities lies at the core of all healthy human development.

During the primary phases of schooling, we take care to develop children's abilities to communicate effectively in oral and written forms. We encourage learners to see other children's points of view, to share and take turns, to understand non-verbal communication, to listen and respond appropriately. We provide role-models of acceptable social behaviour, and discuss, through real-life examples, stories, role play and classroom procedures that illustrate empathy and consider other people's feelings and needs. The development of PSHE (personal, social, health education) lies at the forefront of primary education.

- **Emotional abilities** enable us to understand, share, talk about and deal with our feelings and emotions. They allow us to examine the causes underlying our emotions and enable us to have the courage to change and develop appropriate control. At the highest level, people with well-developed emotional intelligence are engaged in work requiring psychological and psychiatric empathy, understandings and insights.

In primary schools, we spend an enormous amount of time developing an enabling classroom atmosphere, talking to children about their feelings, finding out why children are anxious or afraid, developing self-esteem and confidence, discussing the feelings and reactions of characters in stories, and resolving conflicts and disappointments.

- **Spiritual abilities** relate closely to Emotional and Social abilities. People have an awareness of elements within daily life that are beyond their immediate understanding of the concrete world around them. They search for deeper meanings and purposes, analyse causes and consequences, and seek to interpret 'big' ideas.

Even very young children ask 'big' questions about how the world was made, why seasons come about, and what makes 'things happen'. They want to know about beginnings and how the world works, about intentions and purposes.

● **Linguistic/Symbolic abilities** include all the skills associated with using words – speaking, reading, writing and, of course, listening. They involve using words to create pictures, to reason, to explain ideas, to evoke emotions, to persuade others, to entertain. Verbal abilities are both oral and written, although children are not always equally skilled in both.

There is national concern that many children are entering school with under-developed verbal abilities. Many children lack the experience of being talked to for significant and meaningful periods of time, being read to, rehearsing favourite fairy-stories, learning nursery rhymes and so on. In addition, a significant number of children begin school with a home language that is different from the school language.

● **Mathematical/Symbolic abilities** embrace the use of codes, symbols, numbers, models and diagrams to understand and manipulate mathematical ideas – showing both concrete and abstract relationships. Sign language such as that used by Native Americans, or hieroglyphics such as those on the Rosetta Stone or in the Chinese languages can also be considered as complex representations of ideas in codes and symbols.

Children need to learn the symbolic language of mathematics, beginning with direct life experience and moving on to more abstract manipulation of ideas through mathematical symbols. Mathematical abilities go way beyond numbers: playing with codes, symbols, puzzles, shapes, 2D and 3D game strategies all contribute to the development of Mathematical abilities.

● **Scientific/Realistic abilities** are those needed to explain the real world. These abilities involve the use of observing, identifying, classifying, explaining, and investigating. This cluster of abilities is used to understand systems, relationships, and the natural and scientific world in which we live. Scientists, farmers and therapists all use this collection of abilities.

Teachers engage children in investigative science and are generally skilled in devising 'hands-on' experiments through which children experience real-life problem-solving. However, we need to be careful that children do not learn straightforward scientific fact at the expense of 'doing science' and learning to work in a scientific way.

● **Mechanical/Technical abilities** employ skills that are involved in understanding, manipulating, creating and repairing tools and machines that humans use to perform tasks. All types of Mechanical/Technical abilities involve, in varying degrees, the use of Mathematical, Movement, Auditory and Visual/Spatial abilities. These abilities also include using and manipulating computers and technology. People who have well-developed Mechanical/Technical abilities work with both head and hands. Engineers, designers and mechanics all use this collection of abilities.

Fortunately, the National Curriculum has brought Design Technology to the fore and most early years and primary classrooms make sure that children have opportunities to build, manipulate and make things work mechanically.

● **Visual/Spatial abilities** include not only seeing things accurately and with detail in the physical world, but also seeing things in the 'mind's eye'. Rotating and changing figures, projecting into three dimensions and mentally manipulating images are all characteristics of Visual/ Spatial ability. Artists, inventors, sculptors, architects and mathematicians all use their Visual/Spatial abilities to create feelings, meanings and constructions.

In primary schools, both teachers and pupils take great delight in producing, displaying and discussing visual/spatial products, and classrooms radiate colours, textures and shapes. However, in many homes, children are passively developing their Visual/Spatial abilities: they are often addicted to computer games and television, which demand unthinking reflex action or acceptance, and spend little time creating their own images and deriving pleasure from the doing and making.

● **Auditory/Sonal abilities** (from the Latin 'sonance' meaning sound) enable us to hear, produce and manipulate sounds. We hear external sounds but we also hear sounds 'in our heads'. We hear pitch, tone and expression. Musicians obviously have keen, sensitive Auditory abilities, but poets and writers also have well-developed Auditory abilities that are revealed in their use of rhythm, pattern and alliteration. Public speakers and leaders often use expressive sounds to great effect on their audiences.

Nationally, teachers are sharing their concern about the general lack of listening skills among children, caused in part by their under-developed Auditory abilities: capabilities necessary for an effective teaching/learning interaction.

- **Movement/Somatic abilities** (from the Greek 'soma' meaning body) include all abilities associated with body movement and sensation, including the senses of taste, touch and smell. Gymnasts use gross and fine body control and actors use body language to convey relationships, emotions and feelings. While we all respond and react to our environment through our bodily awareness of taste, touch and smell, some people's senses are particularly acute, for example visually impaired people.

It is of current national concern that many children lack experience in physical play and do not have adequate coordination in gross and fine movement. Many schools are actively seeking to increase the amount of exercise children do and to increase pupils' range of sensory experiences and awareness.

- To what extent are all the human abilities given recognition, attention and status in the current school curriculum?

- How can schools create more opportunities for children to maximise the development of all their human abilities?

Note

See Appendix 1A, which provides a practical teacher observational checklist for general problem-solving abilities, and Appendices 1A.i and 1A.ii, which outline the core characteristics that are specific to each human ability.

What do we mean by learning processes?

Mindmap 4 on p.16 portrays the wide range of learning processes that we all use in different combinations according to the tasks we perform. The mindmap does not portray *all* the learning processes and undoubtedly you will be able to add more. Some learning processes are conscious while others are subconscious. While learners use a unique range of learning processes for every task, inevitably there will be some processes that are common to all learners. The role of the teacher is:

● to teach certain learning processes: for example, there is a range of appropriate recording skills that all learners need to acquire and use, and there are appropriate symbols that learners need in order to decode and manipulate shapes and numbers;

● to create opportunities for learners to exercise learning processes: for example, sensing, reflecting, listening, enjoying, remembering;

● to create a learning environment whereby learners can explore feelings, explore ideas, play and interact.

However, it is also very important to develop tasks and activities in which learners can select and use a range of processes in their own ways.

● Which learning processes do children most often experience in the current school curriculum?

● Which learning processes tend to be neglected in the current school curriculum?

REFLECT

What do we mean by competencies or outcomes?

We want learners to acquire understanding within and across a wide range of competencies developed through school or life activities and experiences. These competencies begin to develop through the first order intuitive knowingness of the young child – such awareness being innate and vibrantly responsive to feelings and sensitivities of safety, comfort, warmth, love and security. The second order development of thinking and problem-solving occurs through immediate, experiential play and sensory learning, when the child becomes more aware of, interprets, and is responsive to the home environment and the reactions of the people within it. This second order development is accompanied by the acquisition of language (verbal and non-verbal) that begins to mediate early experiences and build conceptual, learning frameworks. Third order development of thinking and problem-solving, still mainly experiential, develops through concrete experiences in the wider world. This concrete, practical

Mindmap 3: The range of human abilities

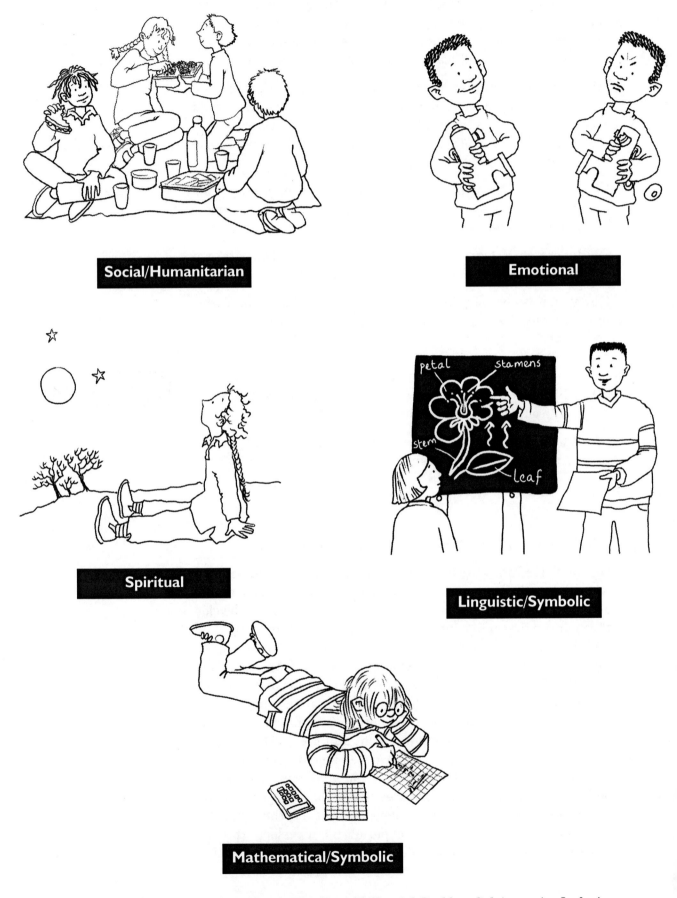

Social/Humanitarian

Emotional

Spiritual

Linguistic/Symbolic

Mathematical/Symbolic

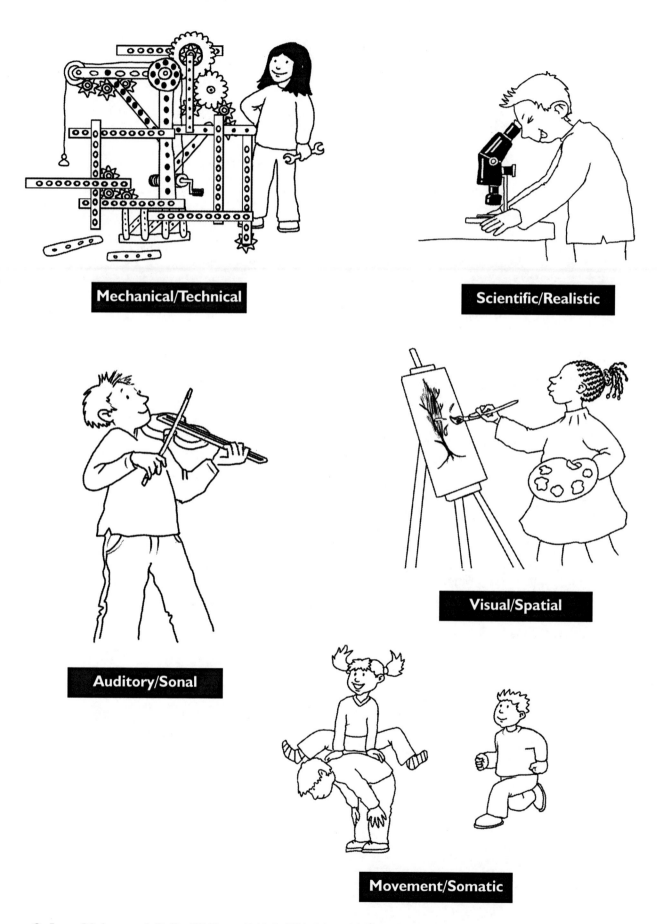

Mechanical/Technical

Scientific/Realistic

Auditory/Sonal

Visual/Spatial

Movement/Somatic

Mindmap 4: The network of learning processes

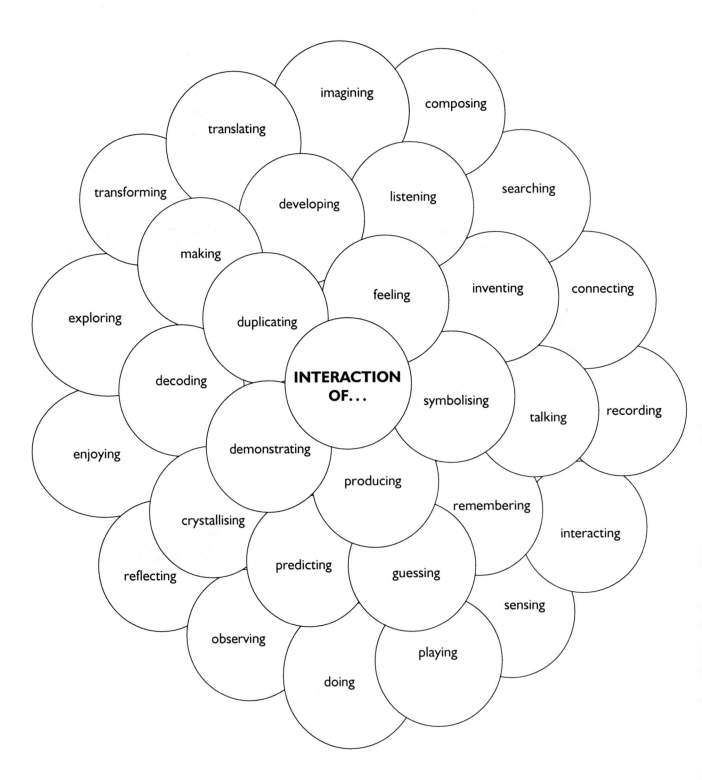

learning enables the child to acquire, understand and use codes, symbols and other representational forms that reveal learning, awareness and communication. The fourth order development of thinking and problem-solving can be regarded as the highest form of human endeavour – thinking in abstract ideas and concepts, and thinking through complex and universal themes and problems.

All people are capable of developing, retaining and using all four orders of thinking and problem-solving in a continuum, moving flexibly and creatively within the four orders to solve problems that range from immediate to long-term, from everyday concrete to abstract and philosophical.

Mindmap 5 shows the evolution of a child's thinking and problem-solving from first to fourth order.

To summarise, learning competencies or outcomes are developed within and across a range of themes which at first need to be embedded in direct, concrete, personal, experiential learning. As learners develop mastery and understanding, the themes need to be widened to embrace issues that become increasingly based in community, national, international and universal contexts. The ideas within the themes thus become more complex and abstract, requiring more advanced thinking and problem-solving.

Mindmap 6 presents a range of themes through which learners need to develop not only a sense of their own independence, but also a realisation of their interdependence within the world scene. Learners also need to develop the confidence and skills necessary to tackle the problems that face them both in their personal lives and as members of a fair and just world.

All the themes can be developed initially within a concrete, experiential framework and they can be gradually extended into more universal and abstract problem-solving activities. For example, resolving conflict in a family environment or an early years classroom can eventually be extended to resolving conflict within an international situation; understanding one's own immediate and personal culture can lead to the recognition and solving of problems in a multi-culture; enjoying and solving problems in the natural environment can result in responsible decision-making with regard to the world eco-system.

Mindmap 5: The continuum of human development from first to fourth order thinking and problem-solving

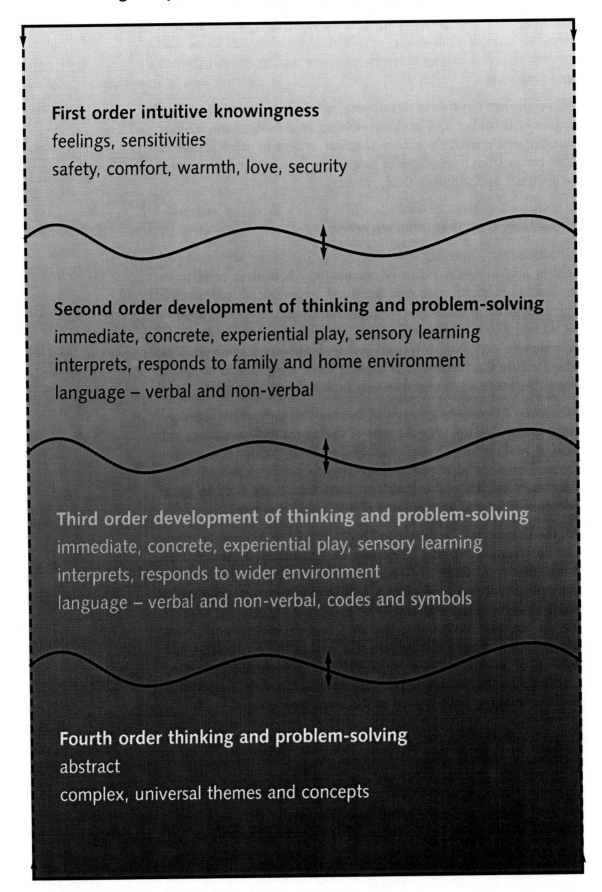

First order intuitive knowingness
feelings, sensitivities
safety, comfort, warmth, love, security

Second order development of thinking and problem-solving
immediate, concrete, experiential play, sensory learning
interprets, responds to family and home environment
language – verbal and non-verbal

Third order development of thinking and problem-solving
immediate, concrete, experiential play, sensory learning
interprets, responds to wider environment
language – verbal and non-verbal, codes and symbols

Fourth order thinking and problem-solving
abstract
complex, universal themes and concepts

Mindmap 6: A range of competencies and outcomes which learners need to develop

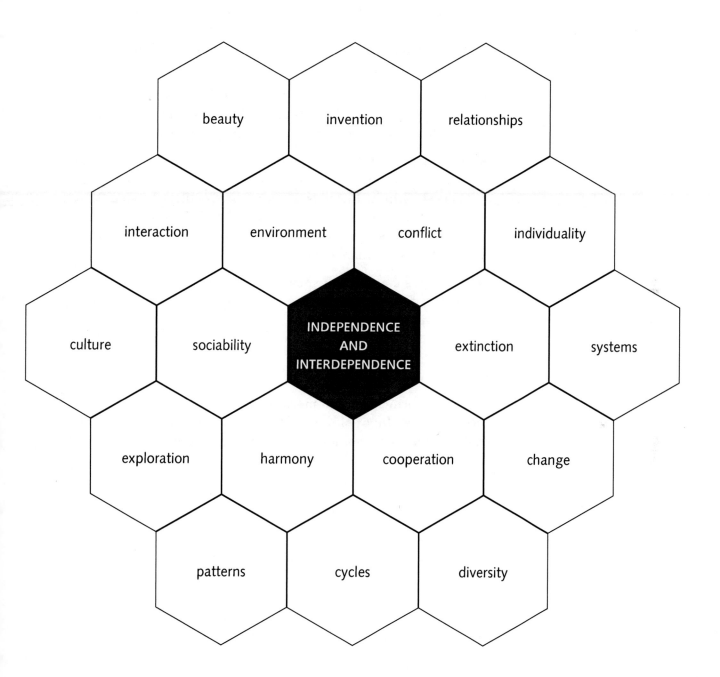

- Which of the competencies and outcomes are included in the current school curriculum?

- Are there adequate opportunities presented for children to identify cross-curricular competencies and outcomes?

So far we have not discussed the essential problem-solving processes that should permeate children's learning activities; nor have we discussed the range of problem types that children should experience.

- Chapter 2 will consider the essential TASC (Thinking Actively in a Social Context) Problem-solving Processes in depth and will provide practical classroom examples.

- Chapter 3 will examine the DISCOVER (Discovering Intellectual Strengths and Capabilities while Observing Varied Ethnic Responses) types of problem-solving that range from closed to open-ended and will show how they can be accommodated within the TASC Framework through practical classroom examples.

- Chapters 4 and 5 will show how all the principles discussed in the first three chapters are put into action in typical primary classrooms.

Note

The major principles summarised in this chapter are further developed by June Maker, Usanee Anuruthwong and Belle Wallace in a future volume that is in preparation.

Summary of Chapter 1: The Rich Spectrum of Human Potential

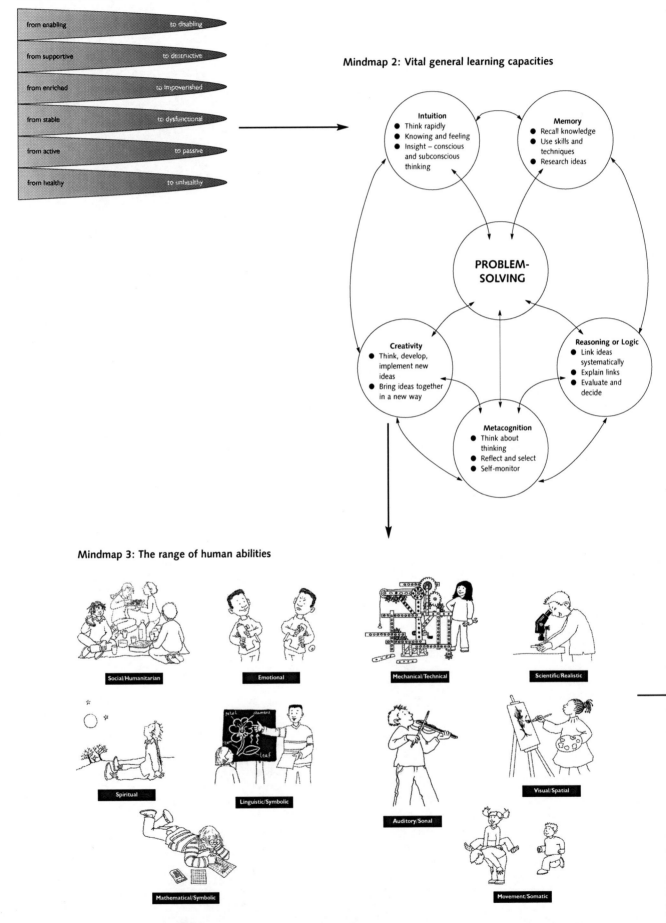

Mindmap 1: The continuum of influential environmental factors

from enabling — to disabling

from supportive — to destructive

from enriched — to impoverished

from stable — to dysfunctional

from active — to passive

from healthy — to unhealthy

Mindmap 2: Vital general learning capacities

Intuition
- Think rapidly
- Knowing and feeling
- Insight – conscious and subconscious thinking

Memory
- Recall knowledge
- Use skills and techniques
- Research ideas

PROBLEM-SOLVING

Creativity
- Think, develop, implement new ideas
- Bring ideas together in a new way

Reasoning or Logic
- Link ideas systematically
- Explain links
- Evaluate and decide

Metacognition
- Think about thinking
- Reflect and select
- Self-monitor

Mindmap 3: The range of human abilities

Social/Humanitarian

Emotional

Mechanical/Technical

Scientific/Realistic

Spiritual

Linguistic/Symbolic

Auditory/Sonal

Visual/Spatial

Mathematical/Symbolic

Movement/Somatic

Mindmap 4: The network of learning processes

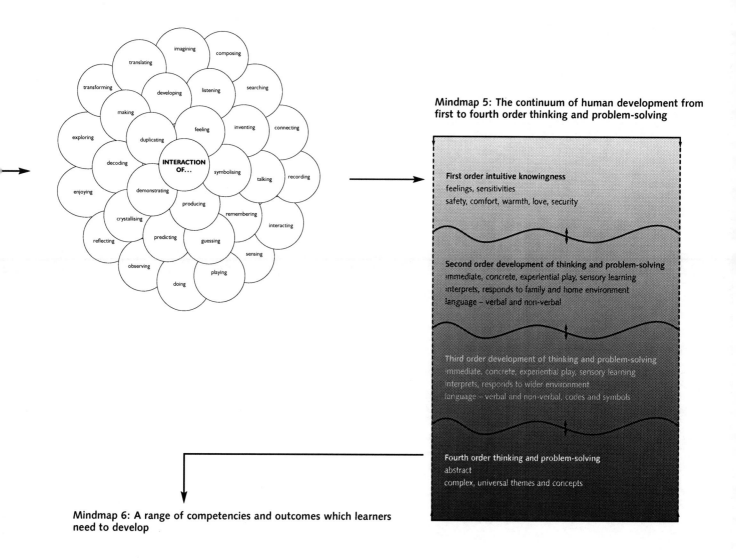

Mindmap 5: The continuum of human development from first to fourth order thinking and problem-solving

First order intuitive knowingness
feelings, sensitivities
safety, comfort, warmth, love, security

Second order development of thinking and problem-solving
immediate, concrete, experiential play, sensory learning
interprets, responds to family and home environment
language – verbal and non-verbal

Third order development of thinking and problem-solving
immediate, concrete, experiential play, sensory learning
interprets, responds to wider environment
language – verbal and non-verbal, codes and symbols

Fourth order thinking and problem-solving
abstract
complex, universal themes and concepts

Mindmap 6: A range of competencies and outcomes which learners need to develop

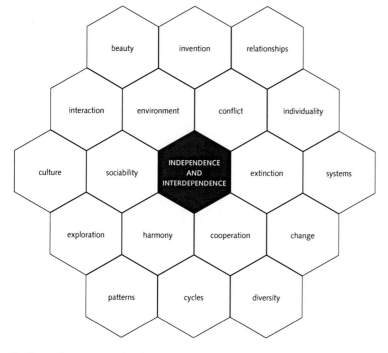

© June Maker and Belle Wallace (2004) *Thinking Skills and Problem-Solving – An Inclusive Approach*, David Fulton Publishers.

Stepping into the Light of the Mind
Teaching the processes of problem-solving and thinking

⭕ ➋ ⭕ ⭕

To enjoy and appreciate the excellence of the mathematician, the dancer, the architect, the athlete, the writer, the leader, the scientist, and the artist, allows us not only the opportunity to bask in the dazzling light of another person's mind, but also in the light of that person's whole being. However, within us all lies the capacity to step into the light within our own minds; and all intuitive, creative, logical and reflective thinking opens the door to that light.

(Belle Wallace)

The purpose of Chapter 2 is, firstly, to outline a universal problem-solving *process* and, secondly, to make the case that *all* children's learning capacity can be improved through the systematic and coherent teaching of the processes underpinning problem-solving and thinking. The writers suggest a cross-curricular model for the development of problem-solving and thinking skills development which is called 'TASC: Thinking Actively in a Social Context'. TASC was initially derived from an internationally based longitudinal action research project carried out with mainstream, multicultural learners, and the TASC Framework has subsequently been used as the theoretical base for a wide range of curriculum development initiatives designed to teach thinking and problem-solving skills. The third purpose of this chapter is to reflect on and extend the theoretical underpinning of the TASC Framework in the light of the principles of learning and teaching outlined in Chapter 1.

Appendix 2 on pages 151–6 provides the following photocopiable sheets:

- 2A   The TASC Problem-solving Wheel (pupils)

- 2B   The Thinking and Planning Guide (pupils)

- 2C   The Tools for Effective Thinking (pupils)

Appendix 2D provides two checklists:

- *Checklist 1* is designed to help teachers assess pupils' problem-solving abilities both formatively[1] and summatively.[2]

- *Checklist 2* can be used by pupils to assess their own problem-solving abilities both formatively and summatively.

Chapter 3 will extend the TASC problem-solving *process* by explaining and outlining the DISCOVER problem *types* ranging from closed to open-ended. Also, Chapter 3 will explain our beliefs about the interconnectedness of creative and analytic thinking, and how these processes combine to activate intelligence in the problem-solving process. We will make a case for including all problem types in the development of creative and analytic problem-solving, a skill and a way of thinking that is sure to become increasingly important in the future.

The meaning of TASC and its essential tenets

Recently, there has been widespread international discussion on the need for the teaching of thinking and problem-solving skills as the key factor in the development of pupils' autonomy, self-confidence and 'learning how to learn' skills, and that all these attributes should be priority targets in schools' development plans. However, we know that teachers have always been concerned with provoking pupils' *thought* during their lessons. Therefore, we emphasise that we are not discussing the *introduction* of thinking and problem-solving skills into classrooms as something that is new; rather we are referring to the need for the auditing, refining and extending of current practice through which all reflective teachers seek to enhance their professional skills. Hence, the purpose of this chapter is to suggest a coherent and universal framework that can be used as the basis for reflection on current practice and for the extension of this framework for the development of a problem-solving and thinking skills

---

1   Formative assessment refers to assessment which provides feedback to the learner during the process of problem-solving so that the learner can respond while she or he is accomplishing the task.

2   Summative assessment refers to assessment which provides feedback to the learner after the problem-solving task has been completed.

pedagogy. We would argue that the major principles outlined in TASC should be reflected in all thinking skills' programmes, although the application of the principles will vary according to the various subject domains.

- THINKING

  The essential message of TASC is that all children are capable of thinking and improving their performance; however, all children need to believe, and know through experience, that they *can* think and are making positive progress in their thinking and problem-solving capacity. This progress needs to be perceived across the full range of human abilities, all of which need to be recognised and celebrated equally. The brain has infinite capacity for thinking.

- ACTIVELY

  Children need to have a sense of ownership of their learning – they need to be actively involved in decision-making. They need to feel significant and to understand not just the *what* of their learning but also the *why*. The brain thrives on active participation and involvement, and this generates motivation, high self-esteem and confidence. In addition, real hands-on learning is dynamic in nature and the brain thrives on active, dynamic, relevant learning.

- SOCIAL

  We talk about the 'I must have it for me now' climate of the technical, quantitative, materialistic world in which we live. The hope for the future lies in the global recognition that, as individuals, we are not just developing from dependence to independence, but rather that we are interdependent in a global community and thus have responsibilities to – and, as a consequence, rights within – that community. Children need to work collaboratively and cooperatively, to practise their thinking and to share ideas with others. Group talk and oracy actively develop the mind.

- CONTEXT

  Children's learning needs to be relevant to their lives, extending from their immediate reality and becoming wider and deeper. They need to understand both the links and the gaps between their home and school cultures, bridging any gap with understanding and confidence. All learners need to see the 'big picture' of their learning – to understand how the 'bits' interrelate and make up a coherent whole. They need to see the relationship between subjects – the common themes, for example: cycles, patterns, relationships, environment (see p. 19).

See Mindmap 7 for an overview of the meaning of TASC and its basic tenets.

 **REFLECT**

● What are the contradictions between the current government demands on teachers and the role of teachers as facilitators of children's emotional and mental growth?

● How can teachers combine the framework of a national curriculum or national standards with a problem-solving pedagogy?

Mindmap 7: The meaning of TASC and its essential tenets (extended from Wallace 2003a)

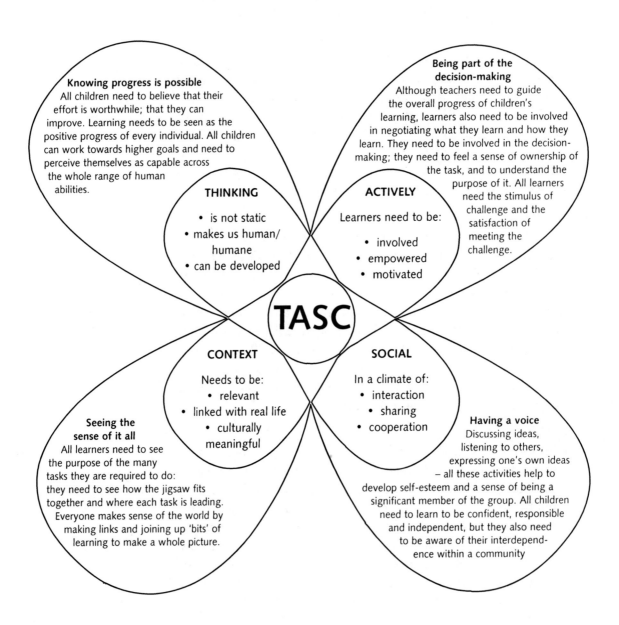

Early seeds from which TASC initially emerged and evolved

The work of Robert Sternberg

Robert Sternberg (1996, 1986, 1985, 1983) has led the way in making the case that intelligence is primarily the ability to use thinking and problem-solving skills in all aspects of life. Importantly, *all* pupils can be taught to improve and extend their working repertoire of skills for planning, carrying out a task, monitoring and reflecting on their progress, and transferring these skills into all other domains. He states that intelligent behaviour involves the processes of adapting, selecting and shaping real-world environments using analytical, creative and practical skills. The levels of all pupils' intellectual functioning can be raised through a curriculum based on problem-solving and thinking skills, although there will obviously still be differences in attainment stemming from the genetic traits and pre-school environments of each individual.

Sternberg analyses the components of intelligence as:

1. *Componential* whereby learners develop skills and strategies (thinking tools) to plan, carry out a task, monitor, reflect and transfer their learning to a wide variety of contexts. The wide range of thinking tools are best acquired when they are first embedded in everyday, real-life and 'fun' contexts that are relevant and meaningful to the learners. The thinking tools need to be given appropriate names and the learners should have specific practice in using them and discussing their usefulness.

2. *Experiential* whereby learners transfer their thinking tools into new situations and content across the curriculum, deliberately recalling the names and previous usefulness. Learners need to be fully aware that they are developing a working repertoire of mental tools that make them more efficient learners, and they need to keep a 'thinking log' in which they record when they use a particular thinking tool. Instead of the emphasis being on acquiring content, the emphasis should be on thinking about the processes of thinking.

3. *Contextual* in which learners adapt, select and shape real-world environments. The school needs to create and celebrate learners as active problem-solvers with an increasingly wide repertoire of thinking tools, and teachers should actively seek as many opportunities as possible for pupils to engage in school and community problem-solving. When working with content that is not immediately related to everyday life, it is essential to find the links between what is being learned and the experience of the learners.

See Mindmap 8 for a summary of Sternberg's theoretical framework.

Mindmap 8: Summary of Sternberg's Concept of Intelligence

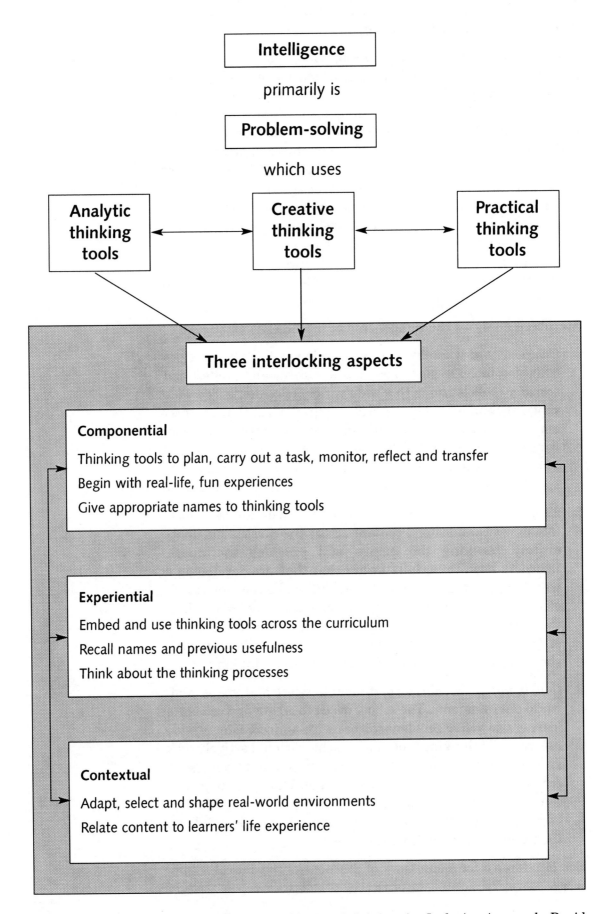

Intelligence

primarily is

Problem-solving

which uses

Analytic thinking tools ↔ Creative thinking tools ↔ Practical thinking tools

Three interlocking aspects

Componential

Thinking tools to plan, carry out a task, monitor, reflect and transfer

Begin with real-life, fun experiences

Give appropriate names to thinking tools

Experiential

Embed and use thinking tools across the curriculum

Recall names and previous usefulness

Think about the thinking processes

Contextual

Adapt, select and shape real-world environments

Relate content to learners' life experience

There is widespread evidence (Brown and Campione 1994; Brown 1987) that learners need to use a wide range of thinking skills both consciously and consistently across the curriculum if such skills are to be transferred into a working repertoire of learning tools. An *ad hoc* scattering of thinking skills across lessons, or an add-on programme separate from the curriculum, does not provide the learner with a comprehensive set of problem-solving and thinking tools that are autonomised and transferred into life.

It makes educational sense, then, to have a coherent, whole-school policy for developing, implementing and monitoring a curriculum that systematically develops a range of problem-solving and thinking tools within real-life situations, across the curriculum and within subject areas. Moreover, we wish to stress that developing a curriculum based on problem-solving and thinking skills not only supports the less able in the development of their potential, but maximises and extends the independent learning skills of the more able. However, working in a classroom that systematically promotes problem-solving and thinking skills inevitably encourages greater differentiation of pupil response; therefore, the ethos of the class, and the whole school, needs to promote a climate of belief in individual quality and acceptance – preferably celebration – of difference!

The work of Lev Vygotsky

Another leading thinker who has contributed greatly to the understanding of how children best learn is Lev Vygotsky (Cole 1985; Vygotsky 1978). Vygotsky confirmed the long-held understanding shared by good, creative teachers that the development of language through guided classroom dialogue, pupil interaction, and the democratic sharing of ideas is not only educationally sound but essential for successful learning. He has stressed that when a teacher-mentor leads learners to negotiate their own meaning and understanding from the base of their own experiential knowledge, then learners are motivated and empowered to learn. Vygotsky also stressed that the route to independent competence is through the initial and sensitive teacher-mentor's 'scaffolding' of the support necessary for the apprentice-learner to gradually become autonomous.

Pupils need to link all new learning with previous learning, finding the conceptual links and extending understanding. They need to see the relevance and the application of their current learning, and they also need to be aware of where the current learning is leading. The brain needs to construct synaptic or neural maps of linked ideas and understanding, thus actively constructing mental pathways. Most pupils forget a great deal when they leap hurriedly from one topic to another without reflection on the purpose of their learning, on the transfer of skills, or the crystallisation of key concepts. Moreover, unless children's learning is firmly embedded in an active problem-solving process, then much of the factual content is lost anyway, and enormous time is wasted both for teaching and learning.

All learners need a rich language base since language is the major medium of communication in the teaching–learning process. Learners need to talk and discuss in order to practise and straighten out their thinking, and the talk needs to begin with their home language before it can be extended to accommodate the 'language of school learning'. Learners also need thinking time and time to negotiate meaning and purpose so that what is being taught and learned has sense and structure.

Vygotsky's ideas are summarised in Mindmap 9.

The work of Albert Bandura and Antonio Damasio

Bandura (1971; 1982) discussed the vital role played by senior learners and adults when they model the desired behaviour for the young learner. Patterns of behaviour are 'caught rather than taught'. Therefore, it is essential for teachers to model and to verbalise their thinking behaviour; otherwise, how can learners reflect back the behaviour through practice, and then make it their own? Moreover, Bandura has also drawn attention to the direct link between positive self-concept and self-esteem, and the motivation needed to persevere with a learning task. Recently Damasio (1999) has confirmed, through neuro-biological research, the close interplay between cognition and emotion, and has underlined the essential role of positive self-concept in successful learning. All learners learn when they are given the opportunity to build on success, and that raises the question of how teachers assess learners' work and how they provide feedback that supports and yet gives guidance for improvement.

Using the broad base of understanding derived mainly from the work of Sternberg, Vygotsky and Bandura, from 1984 to 1993 Belle Wallace and Harvey Adams surveyed the major, worldwide problem-solving and thinking skills initiatives and visited the key projects then currently operating. Adopting an eclectic approach embracing the most successful elements of the range of projects they evaluated, they simultaneously conducted an intensive action research project with mainstream, multicultural learners and their teachers. Problem-solving and thinking skills strategies and methodologies were trialled, evaluated and reflected upon by the researchers, a team of educational psychologists, the participating teachers and the pupils; and gradually a pragmatic working model emerged for the teaching and

Mindmap 9: Development of Vygotsky's Higher Psychological Processes (extended from Wallace 2003a)

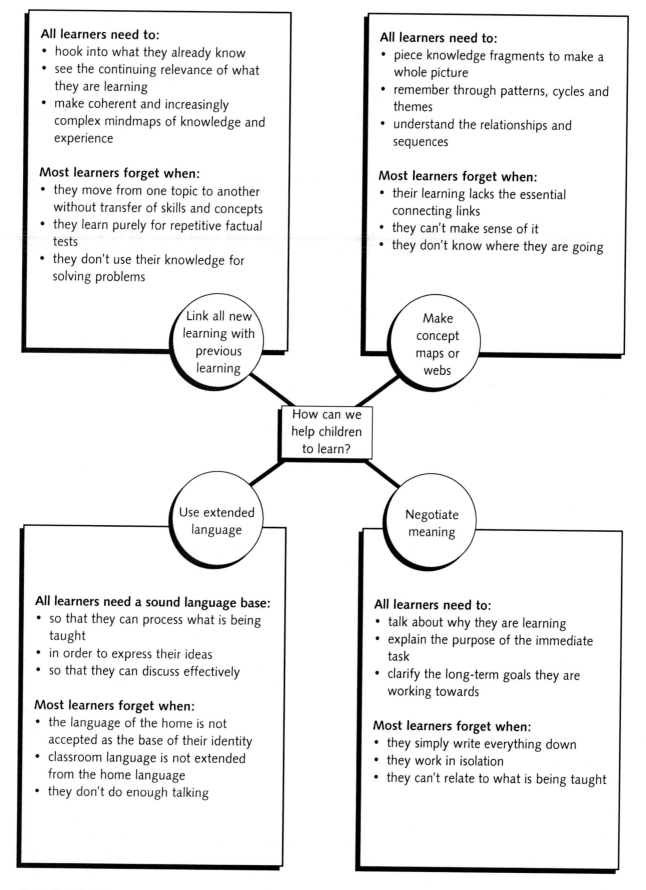

All learners need to:
- hook into what they already know
- see the continuing relevance of what they are learning
- make coherent and increasingly complex mindmaps of knowledge and experience

Most learners forget when:
- they move from one topic to another without transfer of skills and concepts
- they learn purely for repetitive factual tests
- they don't use their knowledge for solving problems

All learners need to:
- piece knowledge fragments to make a whole picture
- remember through patterns, cycles and themes
- understand the relationships and sequences

Most learners forget when:
- their learning lacks the essential connecting links
- they can't make sense of it
- they don't know where they are going

Link all new learning with previous learning

Make concept maps or webs

How can we help children to learn?

Use extended language

Negotiate meaning

All learners need a sound language base:
- so that they can process what is being taught
- in order to express their ideas
- so that they can discuss effectively

Most learners forget when:
- the language of the home is not accepted as the base of their identity
- classroom language is not extended from the home language
- they don't do enough talking

All learners need to:
- talk about why they are learning
- explain the purpose of the immediate task
- clarify the long-term goals they are working towards

Most learners forget when:
- they simply write everything down
- they work in isolation
- they can't relate to what is being taught

learning of thinking and problem-solving skills, and the seeds of TASC grew and blossomed (Wallace and Adams 1993a; 1993b).[3]

Reflecting on and extending the theoretical underpinning of the TASC Problem-solving Wheel

See Appendix 2A for a full-page diagram of the TASC Wheel, and 2B for a full-page diagram of the pupils' Thinking and Planning Guide.

Ten years have passed since the TASC Problem-solving Framework was finalised and published (Wallace and Adams 1993a), so it is appropriate to re-examine the Framework in the light of current thinking and the ongoing practical implementation of TASC in schools. This reflection is based on the principles developed in Chapter 1.

1. The development of vital general learning capacities

Mindmap 2: Vital general learning capacities

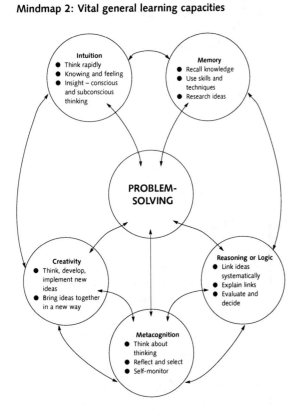

Referring to Mindmap 2 (p. 5), in which the vital general learning capacities are outlined, TASC embraces opportunities for using, developing and improving:

● *Memory* – systematic recall, organisation, and extension of knowledge, use of efficient recording skills and techniques, and research skills;

● *Intuition* – rapid thinking, 'aha!' experiences, acknowledgement of the close link between knowing and feeling, and insight (conscious and subconscious thinking);

● *Creative thinking* – encouragement and development of new ideas, the bringing together of ideas in a new way;

● *Reasoning or logic* – linking and explaining ideas, evaluating and deciding;

● *Metacognition* – thinking about thinking, reflecting and analysing, self-monitoring.

---

3 The principles of TASC were subsequently embedded in a whole-school, multicultural series of Language and Thinking texts entitled *Language in My World* and *Reading in My World* (Cape Town, South Africa: Juta Educational Publishers). Forty-two of the books are currently published (Grades 1 to 9) and six are in press (Grades 10 to 12).

2. Using the full range of human abilities

Considering the full range of human abilities outlined in Mindmap 3 (pp. 14–15), TASC provides opportunities for the development of all human abilities. Primarily, TASC emphasises the importance of the emotional, social and spiritual abilities that drive self-esteem, motivation, self-confidence, positive relationships, and empathy – capacities that are fundamentally important to all learning and living. Additionally, since TASC is designed to be embedded across the curriculum, the remaining human abilities are developed across all subjects and should be equally valued and celebrated. When a school is actively celebrating the wide spectrum of human potential, and every pupil feels that she or he has significance, then it is easier to differentiate activities according to pupils' learning needs.

Mindmap 3: The range of human abilities

Social/Humanitarian — Emotional — Mechanical/Technical — Scientific/Realistic — Spiritual — Linguistic/Symbolic — Auditory/Sonal — Visual/Spatial — Mathematical/Symbolic — Movement/Somatic

Developing learning processes

Mindmap 4 (p. 16) encapsulates the wide range of learning processes that need to be developed with regard to fully activating, using and extending the potential of every child so that she or he can live a fulfilling life; firstly, accepting responsibilities and, consequently, expecting fair and just rights. The major characteristics of this approach take into account the interests, capacities and needs of the learner together with the needs and demands that society will expect from the child. Importantly, the learning process needs to be both enjoyable and appropriately challenging, allowing for both independent thinking and cooperative working. Obviously, learners need to be systematically

Mindmap 4: The network of learning processes

taught a wide range of skills: for example, fundamental routines of literacy, numeracy and information technology, skills of recording, research and communication, and subject-specific skills. This builds up their repertoire of basic tools for learning. Learners also need to use and develop their emotional, creative, and logical learning processes in an atmosphere of acceptance and celebration of diversity and difference. The TASC Framework systematically helps children to be aware of, to reflect upon, and to extend their learning processes. This knowledge of the self develops children's potential to be both cooperative and autonomous learners, recognising their personal strengths and the aspects of the self that need development. The fundamental message is that we learn and develop using all attributes of the self – emotional, social, physical and cognitive; and all human, personal attributes interact and support growth and learning. This growth evolves from first order intuitive knowing, through concrete experiential learning to understanding abstract ideas and concepts.

4. Developing competencies or outcomes

We need to ask ourselves what competencies and understandings children will need to enable them to function effectively in their world of tomorrow. Mindmap 6, p.19, suggests a range of essential competencies and outcomes. We are living at the cusp of a twenty-first century of renaissance and change; we are products of the twentieth century, and we cannot predict with any certainty what life will be like for our children as they mature into adults. The future scenario of possible problems often looks bleak, and, traditionally, curricula are often locked into the scenarios of the past. We certainly need to analyse and reflect on causes and consequences of developments and decisions made in the past, but curricula need to be futures oriented. The competencies children will need lie, for example, in their potential to understand and reconcile cultural differences on a worldwide scale; to cope with fast-moving change; to use new inventions effectively to

Mindmap 6: A range of competencies and outcomes which learners need to develop

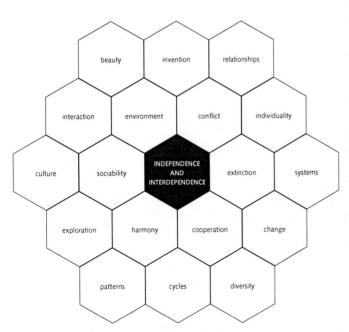

improve life for all; to foster changes in the environment that will ensure its safe survival; to nurture and preserve all that is beautiful and enriching within human cultures. All these competencies are developed through active and real problem-solving; it is through the processes of thinking and reflecting, using all their human abilities, that children will acquire the self-confidence and resilience to function effectively in their world.

Taking TASC on board

Adopting the TASC Approach does not mean a major overhaul of teachers' practice since the skills can be developed incrementally, consolidated and then extended. However, when adopting and developing the TASC Approach in schools, it is more productive and beneficial to develop a whole-school approach so that pupils receive a coherent message across the curriculum.

The overall TASC Problem-solving Wheel is given in Mindmap 10 (pp. 48–9) and the stages are explicit. However, there are certain essential teaching and learning processes that underlie the whole classroom methodology. See Appendices 2B and 2C for the pupils' guides. Pupils need copies of these frameworks to guide their thinking and planning.

TASC teaching methodology

● *Training the brain*

Learners need to understand that they can exercise and 'train the brain' like an athlete trains muscles. Learning and monitoring problem-solving skills, practising and improving them is just like being coached in netball or soccer skills. Learners need to realise that they are not stuck at any set level of performance and talking about their thinking processes and ways of improving them leads to positive growth.

● *Understanding the Problem-solving Process*

Learners should be introduced to the whole TASC Problem-solving Wheel, which they can redesign and fasten into a thinking log-book so that they can refer to the specific strategy they are using. Following the stages of the Problem-solving Wheel consecutively is not always appropriate, and sometimes going back to a stage to clarify the initial thinking is necessary. Learners also need to verbalise the stages of their thinking in order to highlight and crystallise the skills they are practising.

● *Negotiating meaning*

Group work should be used as often as possible so that learners can negotiate meaning and understanding among themselves. A very effective way of establishing peer coaching is to ask learners to explain things to each other. However, group-work skills need to be carefully trained and the purpose of the debate and discussion rigorously established and timed. At the beginning of the training, especially with a class prone to inattention, a few minutes of discussion is sufficient time for learners working in pairs to think of a joint answer or a couple of ideas about an issue. Training in listening skills and taking turns is also important. When reflecting on the thinking process, learners also need to reflect on how well they worked as a team. Sadly, many of today's young people lack the skills of cooperative endeavour because individual 'wants' have been prioritised.

● *Modelling thinking*

When the teacher is leading the learning interaction, she or he needs to verbalise the thinking processes, the thinking language and the stages of the Problem-solving Wheel that are being used. This is essential modelling of thinking skills by a senior learner. Pupils acquire thinking strategies when the teacher first scaffolds the thinking behaviour by giving examples, then gives learners relevant guided practice and gradually withdraws the scaffolding as the learner gains competence.

Working through the stages of the Problem-solving Wheel

● *Gather/Organise: What do I know about this?*

Using and improving the memory is an important part of the whole problem-solving process, and memory works more efficiently and improves when the brain can make links between bits of information.

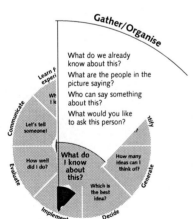

Rather than assuming that learners know nothing about a topic (which we adults often do naturally!), the teacher first needs to gather from the learners what they already know about the topic. A teacher does not need to start a topic off by 'telling' children everything from the beginning. All learners need to bring into their working memory the network of knowledge and ideas they already have. While able learners are often seen to lead the others, a teacher can just as frequently be surprised by an unexpected contribution from a supposedly 'less able' pupil. All the learners' contributions should be recorded quickly in key words or phrases onto a large sheet of paper, and then the teacher needs to encourage the class to make links and group ideas. This collective mindmap helps learners to organise ideas in a coherent way, and the teacher can see the wholeness or fragmentation of the learners' knowledge framework, then refine and extend it. Often, this collective mindmap can be followed by asking the pupils to work on certain aspects to extend the collection of ideas, and to discuss ways in which missing knowledge might be found.

It is also important, at this stage, to discuss the range of learning processes pupils will use or develop, and to examine the major competencies (themes, purposes, concepts) underlying the range of tasks. Groups can then be allocated (or can choose) from a range of tasks that they research, develop and present to the rest of the class. Obviously, this means that learners need to develop a repertoire of research skills and to be clear about the questions they are researching. This way of working can easily occur within the framework of the National Curriculum since many pupils are often repeating skills and knowledge they have mastered. These students need to be taken off the conventional curriculum track and be guided into extension activities.

Auditing what children already know *before completing* fine planning of a topic is the major key to Differentiation of learning tasks. It is even better to find out what children already know and what they would like to find out *before beginning* the broad planning of a topic. This is an essential stage in Assessment *for* Learning.

● *Identify: What is the task?*

Clarifying the task involves both analytical and creative thinking. Many learners lose sight of the task they are undertaking, get lost in detail or are distracted by irrelevant issues, so it is important for them to keep the purpose of the task clearly in mind and to monitor this constantly. Also, many pupils get side-tracked by the rush to produce a quickly finished product that is decorated or coloured as an end in itself, rather than thinking about the purposes and strategies for clarifying, presenting and communicating their ideas. In addition, learners must understand the criteria that will make the task successful or excellent, and have examples of previous pupils' work to discuss and evaluate.

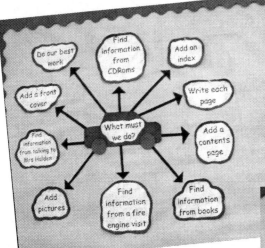

● *Generate: How many ideas can I think of?*

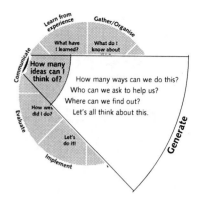

Generating ideas involves high-level creative thinking. Frequently, learners tend to fasten their efforts onto the first idea they think of; many able learners expect the fast and easy completion of a task, while less able learners often cling to the security of the one right answer. So it is important to encourage all learners to stop and think again, or to consider several ideas before deciding on the best idea or course of action.

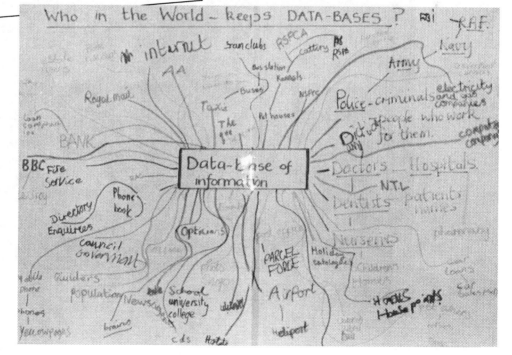

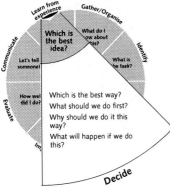

● *Decide: Which is the best idea?*

The dominant thinking tools that come into play at this stage are analytical and evaluative thinking. When making decisions, learners need to prioritise and to give reasons for their choices, rather than deciding impulsively on a course of action or a solution. The course of action then needs to be planned and the possible solution trialled.

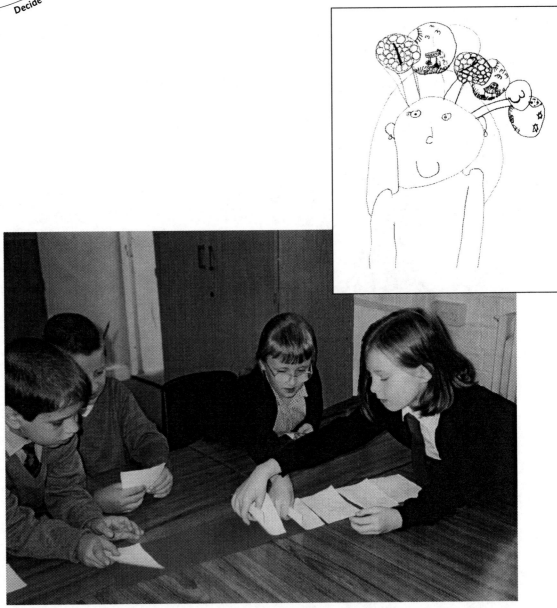

● *Implement: Let's do it!*

We live in a literate, numerate, technical world, and these skills are important; however, children need to express their ideas across the full range of their human abilities as often as possible. To do this, they need to acquire the fullest range of skills in the creative arts, within subject domains, and the world of information technology. They also need to acquire a wide range of recording skills that allow maximum thinking and minimum recording, such as mindmaps, flowcharts, diagram formats and other such displays. Also, pupils need to learn that although Literacy and Numeracy are important, they can develop ideas very powerfully using a wide range of human abilities. Over a term, or a whole year, it is possible to provide opportunities for pupils to use the full range of their human abilities, to develop a wide range of competencies (themes, concepts, purposes) and to use the full spectrum of learning competencies.

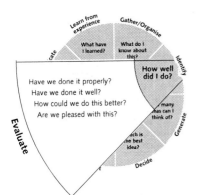

● *Evaluate: How well did I do?*

Children need to be trained in the skill of self-evaluation. Firstly, the teacher helps the learners to talk about the purpose of the task and demonstrates or displays examples of 'good work' across a range of human abilities, eliciting reasons why the work is 'good'. Learners themselves gradually need to establish the criteria that they will use to evaluate their product, otherwise they perpetuate the common practice of 'pleasing teacher' and providing what she or he wants.

The process of evaluation needs to be both formative and summative with learners feeling that every task can be improved because they are learning how to learn.

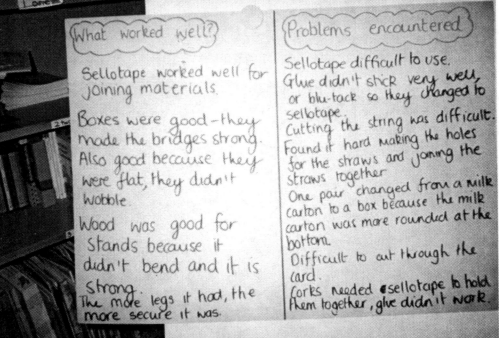

What worked well?

Sellotape worked well for joining materials.

Boxes were good – they made the bridges strong. Also good because they were flat, they didn't wobble.

Wood was good for stands because it didn't bend and it is strong.
The more legs it had, the more secure it was.

Problems encountered

Sellotape difficult to use.
Glue didn't stick very well, or blu-tack so they changed to sellotape.
Cutting the string was difficult.
Found it hard making the holes for the straws and joining the straws together.
One pair changed from a milk carton to a box because the milk carton was more rounded at the bottom.
Difficult to cut through the card.
Corks needed sellotape to hold them together, glue didn't work.

● *Communicate: Let's tell someone!*

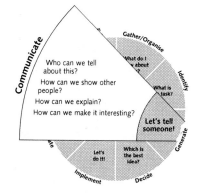

Primary schools are particularly good at creating displays of children's work, and in many primary schools children give talks or performances to other classes. Good though this practice is, there are many opportunities to extend it: for example, older children can be asked to write poems, storybooks and reference books which they or younger children genuinely use, or learners could be encouraged to give demonstrations or performances to teach and communicate to other learners. Pupils need a real audience in order to feel the thrill of communicating and sharing their ideas and the results of their efforts. Also, any presentation of children's work needs to celebrate the stages of thinking and preparation by displaying the evidence of it. Using the TASC Wheel as the centre for the display prompts children to analyse each stage of their thinking and to share that thinking with others. In addition, children looking at the displayed work can see the thinking that went into achieving the final product.

● *Learn from experience: What have I learned?*

The final stage of reflecting is both a formative and summative process that aims at consolidating and transferring what has been learned. This includes reflecting on the major competencies being developed, the learning processes which were used, and the efficiency of the whole problem-solving process. It is also important to reflect on which general and subject-specific skills have been practised, and what important content has been covered. This 'thinking about thinking' or metacognitive stage is vital if learners are to consolidate and transfer skills across the curriculum. An essential question is 'How can we use what we have learned both in other subjects and in our everyday lives?' This is the stage that is usually omitted because teachers come to the end of the lesson and time runs out. And yet it is the most essential stage in bringing about consolidation and transfer of skills. It's a good idea to refer back to the original mindmap constructed in the 'Gather/Organise' stage and to extend it with new knowledge. Doing this enables the pupils to analyse the extension of their knowledge and enables the brain to crystallise what has been learned.

The reader may well comment that the demand of the National Curriculum does not allow time for a problem-solving, thinking skills approach to learning. And, indeed, the National Curriculum is overcrowded with content that has to be covered in a specified time. However, teachers commonly complain that most learners do not remember what they have been taught, so work has to be repeated – and this, incidentally, is a source of great frustration to those pupils who do retain and remember information. We argue strongly that if learners were taught within a problem-solving, thinking skills paradigm, then they would consolidate and remember far more first time round, and the time that is spent on repetition would be considerably reduced. Furthermore, a problem-solving, thinking skills approach develops learners' abilities to learn more efficiently as they acquire and automatise a wide range of learning tools.

The TASC Tools for Effective Thinking

The TASC paradigm incorporates a wide range of Tools for Effective Thinking that feed additional skills into the Problem-solving Wheel. However, in the initial stages of the TASC action research project, a commonly used core of essential Thinking Tools emerged and these are presented in Mindmap 11 (pp.50, 51). See Appendix 2C for a full-page diagram of the Tools for Effective Thinking. Learners need to have a copy of this basic core of Tools which they can redesign, and the teacher needs to create opportunities to introduce and develop skills in using each Tool.

Assessing the development of pupils' problem-solving processes

Teachers are being encouraged to use their professional judgement to make qualitative assessment of children's progress, and this is not difficult with regard to the TASC Problem-solving process. It is important, however, that teachers keep evidence of pupils' thinking together with examples of their planning and the finished product whenever this is possible. This can be in the form of photocopied work, photographs, tape-recordings of discussions, and planning sheets. Equally important is to help learners develop the skills for self-assessment and self-evaluation.

Mindmap 12 (pp. 52, 53) gives a range of criteria that can be used in assessing pupils' work. These criteria can also be shared with the children, and when they are using the processes of the

Mindmap 10: The stages of the TASC Problem-solving Wheel with key teaching principles

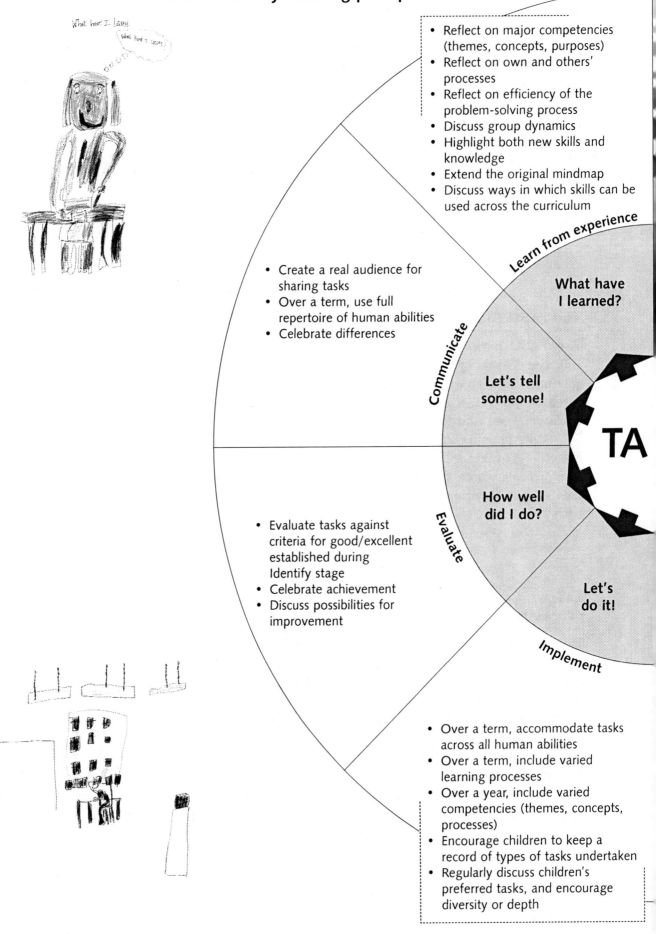

- Reflect on major competencies (themes, concepts, purposes)
- Reflect on own and others' processes
- Reflect on efficiency of the problem-solving process
- Discuss group dynamics
- Highlight both new skills and knowledge
- Extend the original mindmap
- Discuss ways in which skills can be used across the curriculum

Learn from experience

What have I learned?

- Create a real audience for sharing tasks
- Over a term, use full repertoire of human abilities
- Celebrate differences

Communicate

Let's tell someone!

TA

- Evaluate tasks against criteria for good/excellent established during Identify stage
- Celebrate achievement
- Discuss possibilities for improvement

Evaluate

How well did I do?

Let's do it!

Implement

- Over a term, accommodate tasks across all human abilities
- Over a term, include varied learning processes
- Over a year, include varied competencies (themes, concepts, processes)
- Encourage children to keep a record of types of tasks undertaken
- Regularly discuss children's preferred tasks, and encourage diversity or depth

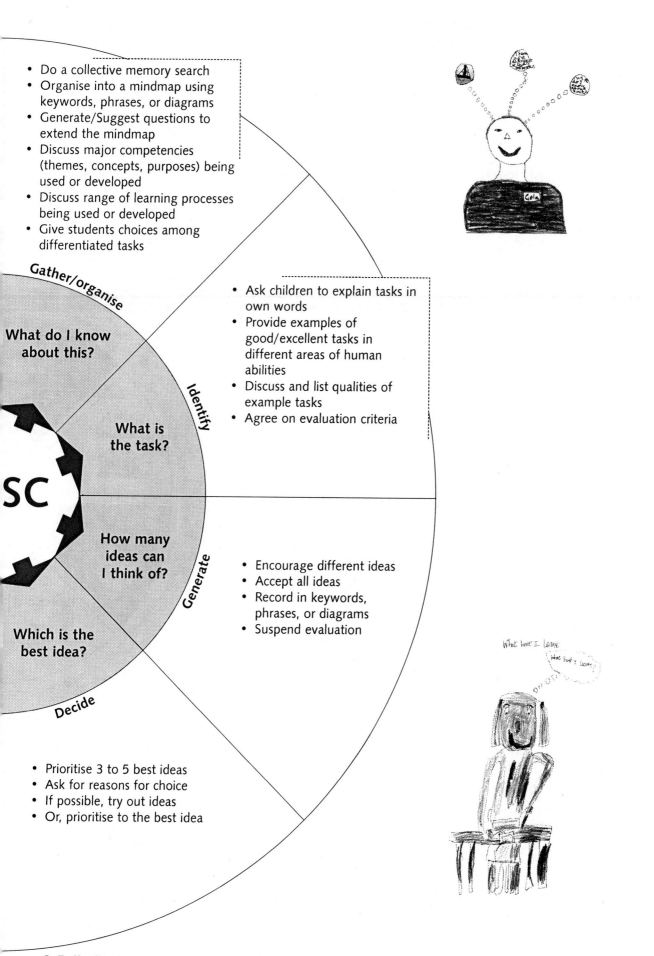

- Do a collective memory search
- Organise into a mindmap using keywords, phrases, or diagrams
- Generate/Suggest questions to extend the mindmap
- Discuss major competencies (themes, concepts, purposes) being used or developed
- Discuss range of learning processes being used or developed
- Give students choices among differentiated tasks

Gather/organise

What do I know about this?

What is the task?

SC

How many ideas can I think of?

Identify

- Ask children to explain tasks in own words
- Provide examples of good/excellent tasks in different areas of human abilities
- Discuss and list qualities of example tasks
- Agree on evaluation criteria

Generate

- Encourage different ideas
- Accept all ideas
- Record in keywords, phrases, or diagrams
- Suspend evaluation

Which is the best idea?

Decide

- Prioritise 3 to 5 best ideas
- Ask for reasons for choice
- If possible, try out ideas
- Or, prioritise to the best idea

Mindmap 11: The Core Tools for Effective Thinking (extended from Wallace 2003b)

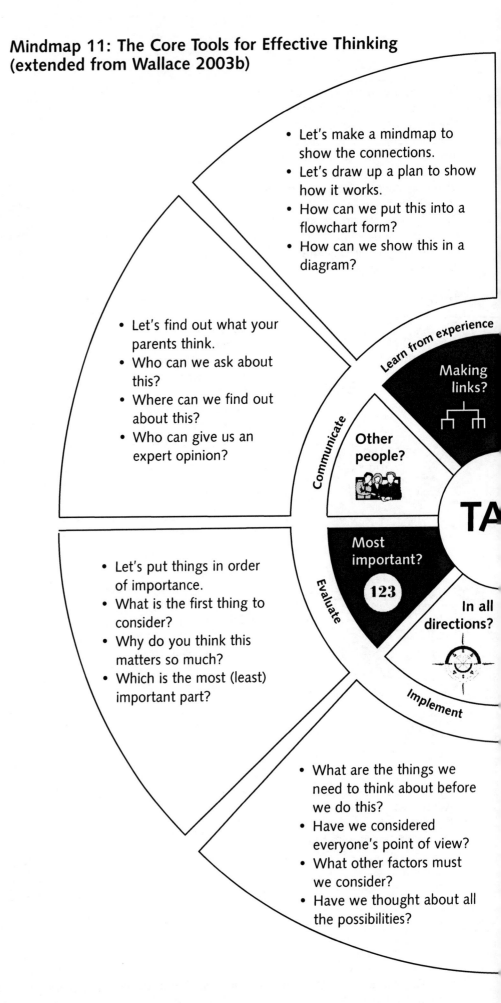

- Let's make a mindmap to show the connections.
- Let's draw up a plan to show how it works.
- How can we put this into a flowchart form?
- How can we show this in a diagram?

- Let's find out what your parents think.
- Who can we ask about this?
- Where can we find out about this?
- Who can give us an expert opinion?

- Let's put things in order of importance.
- What is the first thing to consider?
- Why do you think this matters so much?
- Which is the most (least) important part?

- What are the things we need to think about before we do this?
- Have we considered everyone's point of view?
- What other factors must we consider?
- Have we thought about all the possibilities?

Learn from experience

Making links?

Communicate

Other people?

Evaluate

Most important?

123

TA

In all directions?

Implement

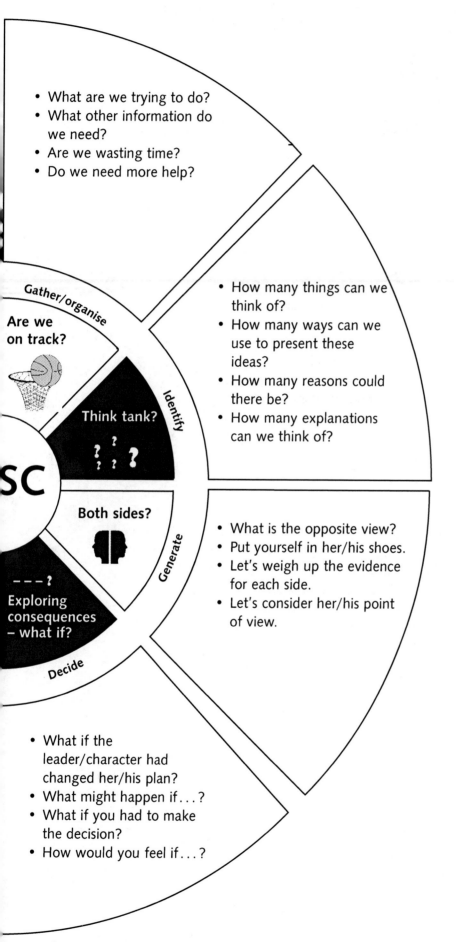

- What are we trying to do?
- What other information do we need?
- Are we wasting time?
- Do we need more help?

Gather/organise

Are we on track?

Identify

Think tank?

SC

- How many things can we think of?
- How many ways can we use to present these ideas?
- How many reasons could there be?
- How many explanations can we think of?

Both sides?

Generate

- What is the opposite view?
- Put yourself in her/his shoes.
- Let's weigh up the evidence for each side.
- Let's consider her/his point of view.

- - - ?
Exploring consequences – what if?

Decide

- What if the leader/character had changed her/his plan?
- What might happen if...?
- What if you had to make the decision?
- How would you feel if...?

Mindmap 12: Assessment criteria for problem-solving abilities (extended from Wallace 2003b)

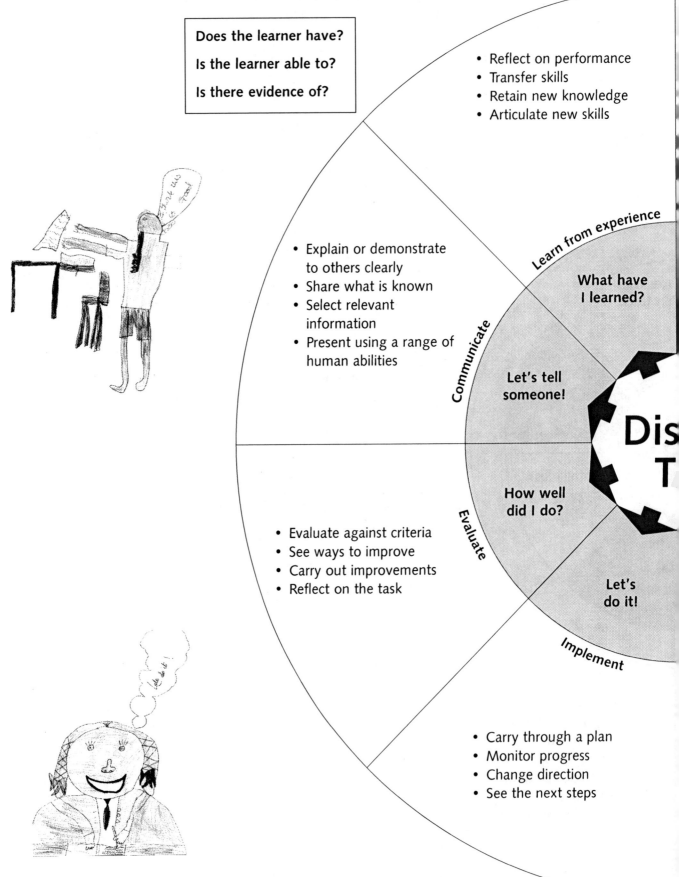

Does the learner have?

Is the learner able to?

Is there evidence of?

- Reflect on performance
- Transfer skills
- Retain new knowledge
- Articulate new skills

Learn from experience

What have I learned?

- Explain or demonstrate to others clearly
- Share what is known
- Select relevant information
- Present using a range of human abilities

Communicate

Let's tell someone!

Dis
T

How well did I do?

Evaluate

- Evaluate against criteria
- See ways to improve
- Carry out improvements
- Reflect on the task

Let's do it!

Implement

- Carry through a plan
- Monitor progress
- Change direction
- See the next steps

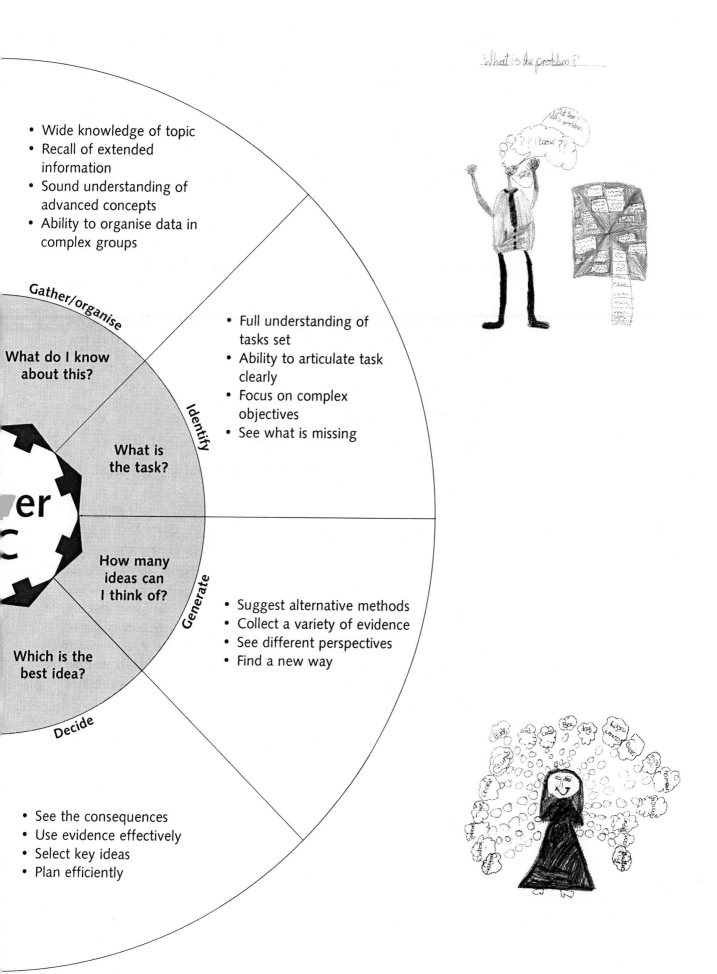

- Wide knowledge of topic
- Recall of extended information
- Sound understanding of advanced concepts
- Ability to organise data in complex groups

Gather/organise

What do I know about this?

What is the task?

Identify

- Full understanding of tasks set
- Ability to articulate task clearly
- Focus on complex objectives
- See what is missing

How many ideas can I think of?

Generate

- Suggest alternative methods
- Collect a variety of evidence
- See different perspectives
- Find a new way

Which is the best idea?

Decide

- See the consequences
- Use evidence effectively
- Select key ideas
- Plan efficiently

TASC Wheel, they can gain the understanding and learn the skills for self-monitoring and review. Appendix 2D encompasses the ten principles which underlie Assessment for Learning as proposed by (Black and Wiliam 1998; Black *et al.* 2004); however, we have aligned these principles with the Problem-solving Process. It provides a checklist for Teacher Assessment of children's problem-solving abilities and a second checklist for pupils' Self Assessment of their problem-solving abilities.

Conclusion

Although curriculum materials aiming to teach problem-solving and thinking skills will vary, this chapter outlines the essential processes that should be incorporated into any programme. Obviously, various disciplines will need to incorporate a range of relevant subject-specific skills and some subjects will emphasise certain aspects of problem-solving more than others. But the following processes must be dominant:

- gathering and organising information;
- clearly identifying the task;
- evaluating the outcome according to specified criteria;
- reflecting on what has been learned and how efficient the learning process has been.

However, we now need to relate the TASC *processes* of problem-solving to the DISCOVER *types* of problems that children should engage with. Chapter 3 examines the range of DISCOVER problems which extend from closed to open-ended. Chapter 3 also includes a discussion of the ways in which ability, and creative and analytic thinking, are interconnected in the problem-solving process. We make a case for including all the problem types to develop skills and ways of thinking that are sure to become increasingly important in the future. We will also show how these DISCOVER problem types relate to the TASC problem-solving process.

Summary of Chapter 2: Stepping into the Light of the Mind

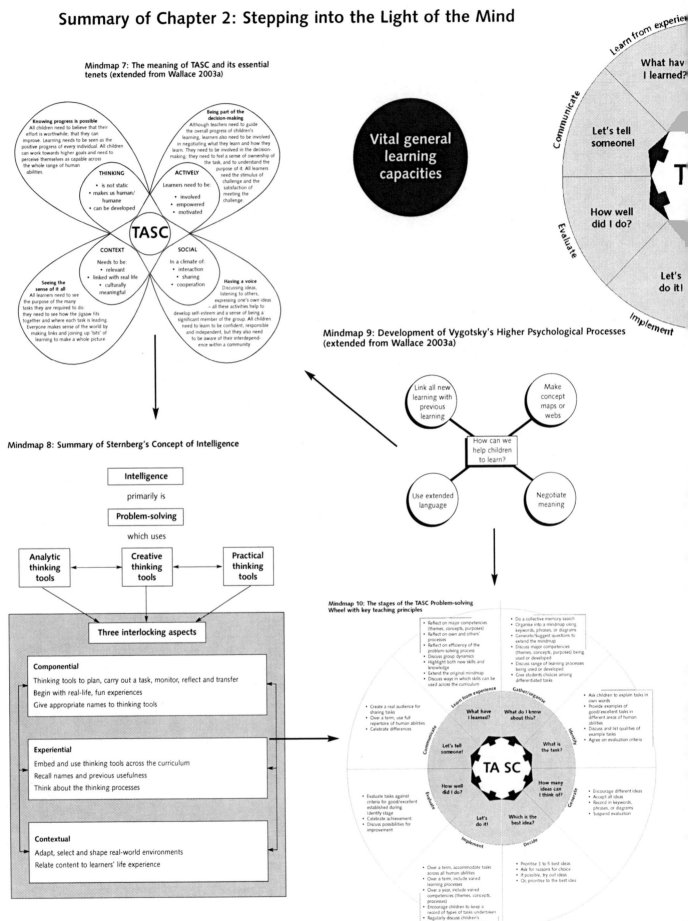

Mindmap 7: The meaning of TASC and its essential tenets (extended from Wallace 2003a)

Knowing progress is possible
All children need to believe that their effort is worthwhile; that they can improve. Learning needs to be seen as the positive progress of every individual. All children can work towards higher goals and need to perceive themselves as capable across the whole range of human abilities.

Being part of the decision-making
Although teachers need to guide the overall progress of children's learning, learners also need to be involved in negotiating what they learn and how they learn. They need to be involved in the decision-making; they need to feel a sense of ownership of the task, and to understand the purpose of it. All learners need the stimulus of challenge and the satisfaction of meeting the challenge.

THINKING
• is not static
• makes us human/humane
• can be developed

ACTIVELY
Learners need to be:
• involved
• empowered
• motivated

TASC

CONTEXT
Needs to be:
• relevant
• linked with real life
• culturally meaningful

SOCIAL
In a climate of:
• interaction
• sharing
• cooperation

Seeing the sense of it all
All learners need to see the purpose of the many tasks they are required to do; they need to see how the jigsaw fits together and where each task is leading. Everyone makes sense of the world by making links and joining up 'bits' of learning to make a whole picture.

Having a voice
Discussing ideas, listening to others, expressing one's own ideas – all these activities help to develop self-esteem and a sense of being a significant member of the group. All children need to learn to be confident, responsible and independent, but they also need to be aware of their interdependence within a community.

Vital general learning capacities

Mindmap 9: Development of Vygotsky's Higher Psychological Processes (extended from Wallace 2003a)

Learn from experience
What have I learned?
Communicate
Let's tell someone!
Evaluate
How well did I do?
Let's do it!
Implement

Link all new learning with previous learning

Make concept maps or webs

How can we help children to learn?

Use extended language

Negotiate meaning

Mindmap 8: Summary of Sternberg's Concept of Intelligence

Intelligence

primarily is

Problem-solving

which uses

Analytic thinking tools ←→ **Creative thinking tools** ←→ **Practical thinking tools**

Three interlocking aspects

Componential
Thinking tools to plan, carry out a task, monitor, reflect and transfer
Begin with real-life, fun experiences
Give appropriate names to thinking tools

Experiential
Embed and use thinking tools across the curriculum
Recall names and previous usefulness
Think about the thinking processes

Contextual
Adapt, select and shape real-world environments
Relate content to learners' life experience

Mindmap 10: The stages of the TASC Problem-solving Wheel with key teaching principles

• Reflect on major competencies (themes, concepts, purposes)
• Reflect on own and others' processes
• Reflect on efficiency of the problem-solving process
• Discuss group dynamics
• Highlight both new skills and knowledge
• Extend the original mindmap
• Discuss ways in which skills can be used across the curriculum

• Do a collective memory search
• Organise into a mindmap using keywords, phrases, or diagrams
• Generate/Suggest questions to extend the mindmap
• Discuss major competencies (themes, concepts, purposes) being used or developed
• Discuss range of learning processes being used or developed
• Give students choices among differentiated tasks

• Create a real audience for sharing tasks
• Over a term, use full repertoire of human abilities
• Celebrate differences

Learn from experience
What have I learned?
What do I know about this?
Gather/organise
Communicate
Let's tell someone!
Identify
What is the task?

TA SC

Evaluate
How well did I do?
Generate
How many ideas can I think of?
Let's do it!
Implement
Which is the best idea?
Decide

• Ask children to explain tasks in own words
• Provide examples of good/excellent tasks in different areas of human abilities
• Discuss and list qualities of example tasks
• Agree on evaluation criteria

• Encourage different ideas
• Accept all ideas
• Record in keywords, phrases, or diagrams
• Suspend evaluation

• Evaluate tasks against criteria for good/excellent established during Identify stage
• Discuss possibilities for improvement

• Over a term, accommodate tasks across all human abilities
• Over a term, include varied learning processes
• Over a year, include varied competencies (themes, concepts, processes)
• Encourage children to keep a record of types of tasks undertaken
• Regularly discuss children's preferred tasks, and encourage diversity or depth

• Prioritise 3 to 5 best ideas
• Ask for reasons for choice
• If possible, try out ideas
• Or, prioritise to the best idea

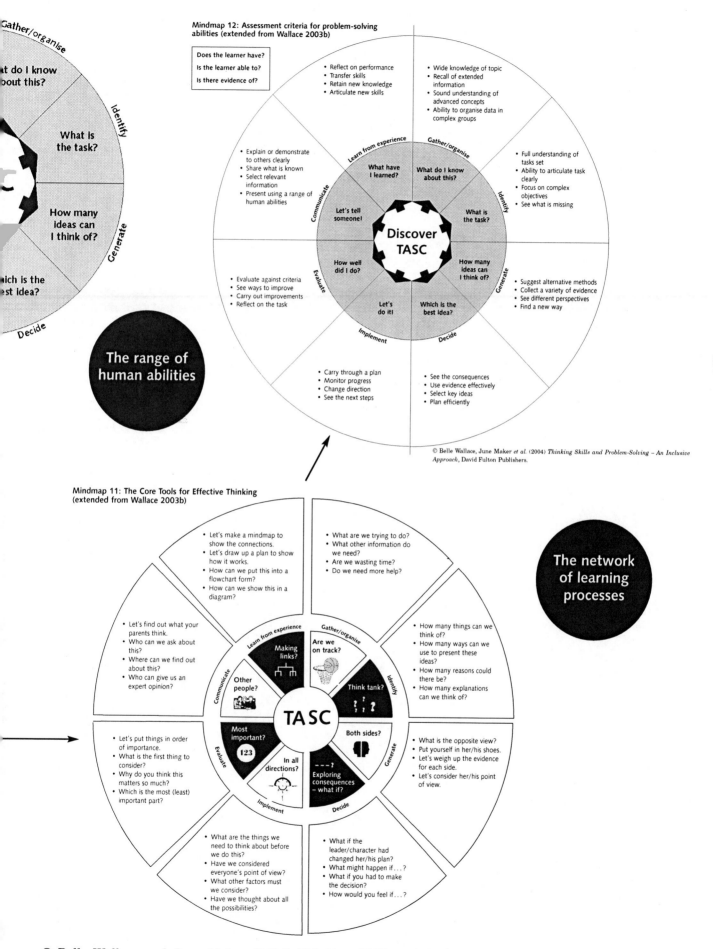

Mindmap 12: Assessment criteria for problem-solving abilities (extended from Wallace 2003b)

Does the learner have?
Is the learner able to?
Is there evidence of?

Learn from experience — What have I learned?
- Explain or demonstrate to others clearly
- Share what is known
- Select relevant information
- Present using a range of human abilities

Gather/organise — What do I know about this?
- Wide knowledge of topic
- Recall of extended information
- Sound understanding of advanced concepts
- Ability to organise data in complex groups

Identify — What is the task?
- Full understanding of tasks set
- Ability to articulate task clearly
- Focus on complex objectives
- See what is missing

Generate — How many ideas can I think of?
- Suggest alternative methods
- Collect a variety of evidence
- See different perspectives
- Find a new way

Decide — Which is the best idea?
- See the consequences
- Use evidence effectively
- Select key ideas
- Plan efficiently

Implement — Let's do it!
- Carry through a plan
- Monitor progress
- Change direction
- See the next steps

Evaluate — How well did I do?
- Evaluate against criteria
- See ways to improve
- Carry out improvements
- Reflect on the task

Communicate — Let's tell someone!

Learn from experience — What have I learned?
- Reflect on performance
- Transfer skills
- Retain new knowledge
- Articulate new skills

Discover TASC

The range of human abilities

The network of learning processes

© Belle Wallace, June Maker *et al.* (2004) *Thinking Skills and Problem-Solving – An Inclusive Approach*, David Fulton Publishers.

Mindmap 11: The Core Tools for Effective Thinking (extended from Wallace 2003b)

Learn from experience — Making links?
- Let's make a mindmap to show the connections.
- Let's draw up a plan to show how it works.
- How can we put this into a flowchart form?
- How can we show this in a diagram?

Gather/organise — Are we on track?
- What are we trying to do?
- What other information do we need?
- Are we wasting time?
- Do we need more help?

Communicate — Other people?
- Let's find out what your parents think.
- Who can we ask about this?
- Where can we find out about this?
- Who can give us an expert opinion?

Identify — Think tank?
- How many things can we think of?
- How many ways can we use to present these ideas?
- How many reasons could there be?
- How many explanations can we think of?

Generate — Both sides?
- What is the opposite view?
- Put yourself in her/his shoes.
- Let's weigh up the evidence for each side.
- Let's consider her/his point of view.

Evaluate — Most important?
- Let's put things in order of importance.
- What is the first thing to consider?
- Why do you think this matters so much?
- Which is the most (least) important part?

Implement — In all directions?
- What are the things we need to think about before we do this?
- Have we considered everyone's point of view?
- What other factors must we consider?
- Have we thought about all the possibilities?

Decide — Exploring consequences – what if?
- What if the leader/character had changed her/his plan?
- What might happen if...?
- What if you had to make the decision?
- How would you feel if...?

TASC

© Belle Wallace and June Maker (2004) *Thinking Skills and Problem-Solving – An Inclusive Approach*, David Fulton Publishers.

Extending the Light of  the Mind

Children today are different, and they are being born into a world vastly different from the world that existed even ten years ago. Change is occurring so rapidly that we, as educators, can no longer simply focus on testing or developing knowledge and isolated skills. We must, instead, provide our children and youth with choices and join with them in creating solutions to the complex problems faced by the increasingly interdependent nations of our world.

(June Maker)

The purpose of Chapter 3 is to extend our discussion of the problem-solving process by integrating June Maker's work on **D**iscovering **I**ntellectual **S**trengths and **C**apabilities while **O**bserving **V**aried **E**thnic **R**esponses (DISCOVER) with Belle Wallace's work on TASC. We will present the continuum of problem types that form the basis of the DISCOVER Curriculum Model – problems ranging from closed to open-ended. In this chapter, our beliefs about the interconnectedness of creativity and intelligence in the problem-solving process will be outlined, and we will make a case for including all problem types in the development of creative problem-solving, a skill and way of thinking that is sure to become increasingly important in the future. Showing how these problem types are related to the TASC processes is also a goal of Chapter 3. Finally, examples of the problem types in all human abilities will show the diversity of experiences we can provide to extend the light of many children's minds to illuminate the world!

Appendix 3 on pages 157–9 is divided into three parts:

● Appendix 3A provides a checklist that presents the analysis of problem types in a summary analysis that is useful for lesson planning.

● Appendix 3B provides a checklist that Upper Key Stage 2 pupils can use to reflect on the types of problems they are solving.

● Appendix 3C presents a menu of activities across the multiple abilities.

REFLECT

● What kinds of problems/challenges do you give children to solve in your classroom?

● What kinds of problems/challenges do your pupils face outside the classroom or school environment (at home, in the street, while playing sports)?

● What kinds of problems/challenges do you face as a professional, a family member, or as a member of your local community?

● What kinds of problems/challenges are faced by the members of our global community?

Research on the DISCOVER Curriculum Model has shown that to develop each human ability to its full potential, and, we would add, to increase the capacity of our nations to participate with understanding and commitment in the global scene, we must emphasise and develop our children's ability to solve a variety of problem types. We must not restrict their work in school to the solving of problems with right answers and known methods, and then expect them to go out into the world and suddenly become capable of creating new products and generating new ideas. We shouldn't forget, either, that this emphasis on open-ended problem-solving is essential for those who are the most highly competent in a particular human ability. These learners are motivated and interested if they are given the challenge of struggling with an unstructured, and often more complex, problem rather than one they know has already been solved.

Here are a few examples of what we mean. During our assessment of Visual/Spatial ability, one 5-year-old may become interested in how she can convince another child to give her something she wants or needs to complete her construction (a *social* challenge) while another 5-year-old is focused solely on how he can make his construction stand up by itself (a *mechanical/technical* challenge). An engineer may become interested in creating a new toy that will capture the attention of children and make money for his company (a *mechanical/ technical* and *social* challenge), while an artist often wishes to find new ways to convey moods and emotions through the use of colours and shapes (a *visual/spatial*, *emotional*, and *social* challenge), and an athlete spends much of her or his time during the early years developing the ability to act with precision, flexibility and beauty to accomplish specific goals (a *movement/somatic* and *visual/spatial* challenge). A musician, on the other hand, uses her or his body with precision to convey moods, ideas and images through the production of harmonious sounds (*auditory*, *movement/somatic*, *social*, and *emotional* challenges). Many scientists and medical professionals spend their entire lives searching for a cure for a previously incurable disease while others wish to map and understand the complexity of the universe (*scientific*, *symbolic/mathematical*, and *spiritual* challenges).

Many teachers already recognise the importance of providing real-life challenges across the curriculum, and often feel that the pressure of teaching 'facts' or standards outlined in the National Curriculum prevents them from preparing children for the complex, ever-changing society in which they will live. In this chapter, we are not suggesting that teachers adopt a completely new way of teaching, and that they abandon the required National Curriculum and standards. In fact, we believe strongly that when varied problems and challenges are given to pupils, rather than problems of only a few kinds, children and youth will learn the National Curriculum and achieve the national standards more quickly and permanently – and that both the teacher and the pupils will have much more fun learning!

All teachers provide a range of problem-solving situations or challenges for their pupils. However, sometimes we get into a 'rut' and focus on only certain types or problems in certain content areas or in certain areas of human abilities. In this chapter, we will outline a framework for examining the variety of problem-solving situations you already provide, and then suggest ways to extend what you do into other areas of the curriculum, exploring other human abilities and presenting problem situations that are new to you and your pupils.

Overview of DISCOVER

● DISCOVERING
  One of the most important ideas in this model is that all of us must realise that we do not know everything there is to know about our pupils, ourselves, or the world. Scientists are always making new discoveries about the natural world; psychologists are always discovering new ways that the mind works; our pupils amaze or disappoint us (depending on our perspective!); and living in this world is a constant growing and learning experience as we discover our own hidden feelings, fears and talents.

● INTELLECTUAL STRENGTHS and CAPABILITIES
Another key idea in DISCOVER is that everyone has a wide range of intellectual abilities – humans are not 'intelligent' or 'retarded' as many people at the turn of the century believed. All of us possess at least ten different types of abilities, and what makes us unique is our particular *pattern* of these abilities: we are interested in and have opportunities to develop some of them, and are not interested in or do not have opportunities to develop others. We naturally inherit a higher potential or capacity for some abilities than we do for others. This interest, combined with opportunities and inherited capacity, results in our individual profile of abilities.

● OBSERVING
The best way to discover the strengths and capabilities of all the pupils in our classes, of our own children and family members, of ourselves and those from cultures vastly different from our own, is to observe – to use our natural capacity for watching. There are times when it is necessary to watch without interfering while children play or interact: we might observe the effects of a new teaching technique, or structure a learning situation so that we can see if children can use certain skills we have taught, and we score or note pupils' responses to the tests we administer. All of us are 'inside looking out' in the sense that we are viewing the world from our own perspective. We have a certain philosophy, particular values, and a whole host of personal experiences that shape what we *think* about what we see, as well as what we actually 'register' in our minds from the many sights, sounds, odours and tastes in the environment. All of us can refocus our lenses as well as widen their scope so that we discover the richness and beauty of each child we see.

● VARIED ETHNIC RESPONSES
Embedded in this phrase are two important ideas: respecting and valuing the responses of children from different ethnic, cultural, and linguistic backgrounds; and giving equal respect and value to responses of children with different patterns of human abilities. Many of our testing instruments penalise children who are creative – children who think differently about a problem or answer a question differently from the expected or 'correct' answer in the test manual. Unfortunately, this penalty is often applied in the classroom as well. Pupils whose answers seem to be 'off track' are ignored or are told they are 'wrong' without being questioned about how their answer or response is related to the question being asked. Children from diverse ethnic, cultural, and linguistic backgrounds often have experiences and knowledge that are different from their 'mainstream'

peers and teachers. All too frequently, these differences are perceived as deficits and the children are viewed as being incompetent, or as less competent than their 'mainstream' peers.

Theoretical Background to DISCOVER

In the DISCOVER Projects, June Maker and Shirley Schiever began the research by investigating how Howard Gardner's 'Theory of Multiple Intelligences' (Gardner 1983; 1993) could be applied. They found this to be a particularly attractive theory since it includes the idea that many intelligences, not just one, can be found in people. The theory also includes the important concept that the same intelligence can be expressed differently, based on the person's cultural background and perspective. An equally important factor to us was that Gardner had developed clear and defensible criteria for determining and distinguishing between the domains or areas that he was willing to label 'intelligences', and these 'intelligences' made sense in both a practical and theoretical way.

Perhaps the most significant idea of Gardner's that excited us was his general definition of intelligence: 'Human intellectual competence must entail a set of skills of problem-solving enabling the individual to resolve genuine problems or difficulties . . . and must also entail the potential for finding or creating problems – thereby laying the groundwork for the acquisition of new knowledge' (Gardner 1983, pp. 60–1). By using this definition, he set the stage for us to view intelligence very differently from the way it was perceived in the early 1900s when IQ tests were first being developed. We could now look at 'intelligence' and 'creativity' as two aspects of the same construct – not two different constructs.

We drew on the work of researchers Getzels and Csikszentmihalyi (1967; 1976), who categorised problems (challenges) according to the amount of information given or known by the person who presents the problem and the person who is expected to solve it. Essentially, this is a continuum of problem-solving situations beginning with the most 'closed' and ending with the most 'open'. In the scheme developed by Getzels and Csikszentmihalyi, three problem types were included. We first added two more to complete the gap between their first and third, and have recently added one more (Maker and Schiever, in press; Schiever and Maker 1991; 1997). At this point it is important to stress that it is easy to see the difference between a Type 1 problem (closed) and a Type 6 problem (open): however, the problem types form a continuum and the boundaries between consecutive problems may be blurred. Often it is the actual wording the teacher uses to communicate the activity to the group of learners that puts the activity into a specific type.

Mindmap 13 provides an analysis of problem types along the continuum from closed to open-ended. This analysis is useful for lesson planning and enables teachers to ensure that they are presenting learners with a range of problem types. (Chapter 4 shows how this analysis has been put into practice in lesson planning.)

To connect the ideas of Gardner and the research of Getzels and Csikszentmihalyi with the constructs of creativity and intelligence, we examined different tests designed to measure intelligence and creativity, and found that the overwhelming majority of tests of intelligence (and also tests of achievement and critical thinking) include only Problem Types 1 and 2 – the closed problems. Tests of critical thinking include some Type 3 problems. On the other hand, all except one test of creativity include only Problem Types 4 and 5 – the open-ended problems. For instance, Type 4 problem situations have a clearly defined problem, but several methods and several solutions are appropriate. Type 5 problem situations have a clearly defined problem but an unlimited number of methods and solutions can be found. The number of appropriate methods and solutions to Type 5 problems is limited only by the solver's imagination and knowledge. Thus, we believe researchers have made an artificial distinction between creativity and intelligence by assessing them using different types of problems. Unfortunately, the most open-ended type of problem (Type 6), one in which the solver must first define the problem to be solved, is not used in any current tests of creativity, even though it has been an important part of research on creativity.

Mindmaps 14 and 15 provide practical examples of how the full range of problem types have been built into broad thematic topics – 'Toys and Games' (Key Stage 1) and 'Ancient Egypt' (Key Stage 2). The over-arching themes of 'Toys and Games' are: Children's Games; Friendship, Love and Relationships. The over-arching themes of 'Ancient Egypt' are: Ancient Culture; Ethics and Systems. In developing thematic topics, it is important to highlight the theme as often as possible. Also, the problem types have been analysed across the full range of multiple abilities. Obviously not all the activities would be developed in either thematic topic, but the mindmaps provide a full menu of problem types and activities from which teachers can make selections over a full year.

The key idea in the DISCOVER research and practice is that intelligence and creativity are not different, but are both *adaptive, appropriate responses to different types of challenging*

Mindmap 13: Analysis of DISCOVER problem types

	Type 1	Type 2	Type 3	Type 4	Type 5	Type 6
Specific thinking skill	• Meet a specific goal • Solve a well-defined problem • Use a known technique • Practise a new strategy • Get the correct answer	• Meet a specific goal • Solve a well-defined problem • Choose/Apply the right method for the problem • Decide when to use certain methods • Get the correct answer	• Meet a specific goal • Solve a well-defined problem • Create/Use many ways to meet a goal or solve a problem • Create new methods or use known methods in different ways • Get a correct answer	• Meet a specific goal • Solve a well-defined problem • Create/Use your own way(s) to meet a challenge • Create your own solution(s) to a problem • Choose the best method (using specified criteria) • Choose the best solution (using specified criteria)	• Meet a specific goal • Solve a well-defined problem • Create/select way(s) to solve a problem • Create/select solution to a problem • Choose the best method (using your own criteria) • Choose the best solution (using your own criteria)	• Decide on an issue you would like to explore (not clearly defined) • Meet a personally-identified challenge • Establish own goals • Create/select way(s) to meet the challenge • Create/select own solution to the problem • Choose the best method (using your own criteria) • Choose the best solution (using your own criteria)
Justification	• Helps pupils practise their learning • Develops a knowledge base • Helps teachers know if their pupils have learned to apply a method that was taught	• Helps pupils develop skills in deciding on appropriate problem-solving methods • Develops knowledge and skills • Helps teachers know if pupils can select the best or most effective way to reach a solution	• Helps pupils develop creative thinking about methods for solving problems • Increases knowledge and skills • Helps teachers know if pupils can combine logical and creative thinking in a goal-directed way	• Helps pupils develop the ability to apply known criteria to make decisions • Increases creativity, flexibility, and divergent thinking abilities within limits of a particular curriculum standard, content area, or topic • Helps teachers move pupils from 'consumers' of knowledge to 'producers' of knowledge	• Helps pupils develop decision-making skills • Increases creativity, flexibility, and divergent thinking abilities across curricular areas or standards • Provides for integration of knowledge and skills from many curricular areas • Helps teachers see how pupils use their knowledge in different ways to reach their own solutions	• Helps pupils develop decision-making skills • Increases creativity, flexibility, and divergent thinking abilities across curricular areas or standards • Provides for integration of knowledge and skills from many curricular areas • Helps teachers see how pupils use their knowledge in different ways to reach their own solutions • Increases pupils' ownership of learning and problem-solving • Increases motivation for high-ability pupils • Helps pupils prepare for challenges and problems in real-life situations • Increases pupils' ability to see and sort through the complexity of personal, local, and global problems

Mindmap 14: Using problem-solving activities 1 to 6 across the multiple abilities
EXPLORING TOYS AND GAMES: Foundation Phase

	Type 1: Clearly defined; Known method; Correct answer	Type 2: Clearly defined; Select method; Correct answer	Type 3: Clearly defined; Create method; Correct answer	Type 4: Clearly defined; Create method; Best answer; Specified criteria	Type 5: Clearly defined; Unknown method; Best answer; Own criteria	Type 6: Not clearly defined; Unknown method; Best answer; Own criteria
1 Social	Let's make a tick-chart showing all the reasons we like Teddy Bears.	Let's make a block graph to see which are our most favourite games.	Let's make an invitation to our Teddy Bears' Picnic.	Let's make a leaflet about our Teddy Bears' picnic.	Let's plan and practise all the games we will play on our Teddy Bears' Picnic.	Let's plan a Teddy Bears' Picnic. What are the most important things to think about?
2 Emotional/Personal	Watch a puppet show.	Tell about the feelings of the puppets in the show.	Why do you think the puppets felt that way?	If this puppet was angry, what are the ways it could become more peaceful?	If you were angry, how could you change your feelings.	Make a mask or a puppet show about feelings.
3 Spiritual	How would you feel if you lost your favourite toy? How would you feel when you found it?	Let's draw pictures of happy and scary toys.	Why do Teddy Bears make us feel good?	Let's make a display of all the toys that make us feel the happiest.	Let's make a toy or a game that makes a sad person happy.	Let's make a toy or a game about our lives.
4 Linguistic/Verbal	Which are our favourite toys?	Let's compare old and new toys.	Let's make a list of all the things that a very special toy should have.	Which toy would you like to take on holiday? Why would you take it?	In how many ways can we improve this toy?	Tell me about the new toys you would like to have.
5 Mathematical	Let's measure and weigh all our toys and put them in order.	Let's draw a Venn diagram to show what is the same and different about new and old toys.	How many ways can we sort the toys into groups?	Let's invent a counting game about toys.	Which counting game do you like the best? Why?	Let's make a dance about numbers.

Mindmap 14: Using problem-solving activities 1 to 6 across the multiple abilities

EXPLORING TOYS AND GAMES: Foundation Phase

		Type 1: Clearly defined; Known method; Correct answer	Type 2: Clearly defined; Select method; Correct answer	Type 3: Clearly defined; Create method; Correct answer	Type 4: Clearly defined; Create method; Best answer; Specified criteria	Type 5: Clearly defined; Unknown method; Best answer; Own criteria	Type 6: Not clearly defined; Unknown method; Best answer; Own criteria
6	Scientific	Where are the best places to have picnics? Why?	What First Aid might we need?	Let's find out the best way to store the food for our picnic.	Let's decide how we will make our food.	Let's advertise our 'healthy picnic'.	Let's plan and organise our class picnic.
7	Mechanical/ Technical	Put together a model of a plaything in a park (pieces are given).	Let's group all the playthings we would find in a park.	Let's compare the models made by all children in our class.	Let's draw a swing for the park.	Let's build a model of our swing.	Let's make a model of our own fun-park.
8	Visual/ Spatial	Let's draw a picture of Barnaby Bear.	Let's find pictures of toys and put them into groups.	Let's make a jigsaw puzzle from a picture of a toy.	Let's design a poster to advertise our moving toy.	Let's draw a moving toy for the future and label the parts.	Let's invent a shape game using shapes.
9	Musical/ Auditory	Play this rhythm on your instrument.	Let's listen to different kinds of music and say whether it is 'going to sleep' music or 'waking up' music.	Let's listen to some music and say which story it would match.	How many happy and sad musical sounds can we make for our toys?	Let's be toys in a tea party.	Let's choose the sounds we like the best and make up a song.
10	Movement	Let's make toy-walks to the beat of the music.	Let's use every part of our bodies while we move to the beat of the music.	Let's do our movements in slow motion like a robot.	Let's join up all our movements to make a dance.	Let's make up dances to different kinds of music.	Let's invent our own dance.

Note: It is easy to see the difference between Problem Types 1 (closed) and 6 (open). However, the problem types form a continuum from 1 to 6, and it is often the *way that the problem is worded* that distinguishes the types.

Mindmap 15: Using problem-solving activities 1 to 6 across the multiple abilities

HISTORY – Ancient Egypt: Key Stage 2

		Type 1: Clearly defined; Known method; Correct answer	Type 2: Clearly defined; Select method; Correct answer	Type 3: Clearly defined; Create method; Correct answer	Type 4: Clearly defined; Create method; Best answer; Specified criteria	Type 5: Clearly defined; Unknown method; Best answer; Own criteria	Type 6: Not clearly defined; Unknown method; Best answer; Own criteria
1	Social	Ask your friend to tell you three facts about Ancient Egypt.	Make a class calendar to illustrate the Egyptian festivals.	Make a class book to teach other classes about Ancient Egypt.	Organise a group debate about the 'good' and 'bad' things in Ancient Egypt.	Write and produce a play about your life and feelings as an Egyptian queen.	Investigate the law system of Egypt.
2	Emotional/ Personal	Describe how you felt as you read about Ancient Egypt.	Tell why you felt this way as you read about Ancient Egypt.	Which aspects of Egyptian life do you like best? Why?	Write a poem to describe your life as a slave.	Do you think the Egyptian way of life was fair to everyone? Why? Why not?	Investigate the emotional life of an Egyptian person. How were feelings influenced by your places in society?
3	Spiritual	Compare the religion of Ancient Egypt with a religion of today.	Draw a chart that shows the different beliefs of the people of Ancient Egypt.	How would you have changed the lives of the slaves?	Make a display to show the 'good' beliefs and the 'bad' beliefs of people in Ancient Egypt.	What do you think about the religious beliefs of Ancient Egypt?	Which of the problems of living in Ancient Egypt would you choose to solve? How would you do this?
4	Linguistic/ Verbal	Write a story about the life of Howard Carter.	Write a letter to an Egyptian child explaining how your life is different from his or hers.	If you were Pharaoh, how would you have treated the slaves?	Produce an Egyptian newspaper.	Invent a new language.	Organise a debate about some aspect of Ancient Egypt.
5	Mathematical	Make a flow chart to show a day in the life of a priest.	Draw a Venn diagram to show similarities and differences between the present day and Ancient Egyptian times.	Invent an Ancient Egyptian counting game.	Make a flowchart to show how all aspects of life in Ancient Egypt were related.	Create a display to show the work of an archaeologist.	Explore the mathematics of Ancient Egypt.

Mindmap 15: Using problem-solving activities 1 to 6 across the multiple abilities

HISTORY – Ancient Egypt: Key Stage 2

	Type 1: Clearly defined; Known method; Correct answer	Type 2: Clearly defined; Select method; Correct answer	Type 3: Clearly defined; Create method; Correct answer	Type 4: Clearly defined; Create method; Best answer; Specified criteria	Type 5: Clearly defined; Unknown method; Best answer; Own criteria	Type 6: Not clearly defined; Unknown method; Best answer; Own criteria
6 Scientific	Describe the climate in Egypt.	Make a chart to compare the animal life of Ancient Egypt and Britain today.	Plan an Ancient Egyptian herb garden.	Make an exhibition of the most effective medicines of Ancient Egypt.	Compare the medicines used in Ancient Egypt and today.	Investigate the science of Ancient Egypt.
7 Mechanical/Technical	Investigate how the pyramids were constructed.	Sketch the important parts of Ancient Egyptian machines.	Make a replica of an Ancient Egyptian machine.	Make a display to show parts of Ancient Egyptian machines that are still used in machines today.	Build a model of an Ancient Egyptian village.	Invent and make a machine that could have been used in Ancient Egypt.
8 Visual/Spatial	Recreate an Ancient Egyptian work of art.	Draw a map of the world at the time of Ancient Egypt.	Sketch the main scenes in a TV programme about Tutankhamen.	Design some 'modern' Egyptian clothes based on Ancient Egyptian styles.	Create a picture game to teach about Ancient Egypt.	Design an exhibition about Ancient Egypt.
9 Musical/Auditory	Record some Egyptian music to play to your class.	Create the sounds of a typical Egyptian market.	Make an audio-tape using only sounds to explain the embalming process.	What music would you choose to represent Pharaoh, a priest, a slave, a dancer?	Decide on the background sounds to go with your story.	Invent your own Egyptian music.
10 Movement	Make a puppet dressed in Egyptian costume.	Make a model of an Egyptian boat.	Perform an Ancient Egyptian dance.	Make up a courtroom trial of a slave who stole food.	Create your own Egyptian dance.	Role-play life in Ancient Egypt and today.

Note: It is easy to see the difference between Problem Types 1 (closed) and 6 (open). However, the problem types form a continuum from 1 to 6, and it is often *the way that the problem is worded* that distinguishes the types.

situations. Often, different types of challenging situations result from the different goals of the individual who presents the problem situation. In a school setting, a maths teacher may be interested in knowing if a pupil has learned her maths facts, so she or he presents a problem for the pupil to solve: $3 + 5 = ?$ (a Type 1 problem if the child knows how to add). Another maths teacher may be interested in knowing if a pupil can think of many different ways to calculate the area of a rectangle that is 4 inches by 9 inches, so she presents a Type 3 problem for the pupil to solve.

In reality, most of us solve a variety of problems (meet a variety of types of challenges) every day, and that is what the problem continuum is designed to call to our attention. Obviously, the boundaries between consecutive problem types will be blurred, i.e. between Types 1 and 2 or between Types 5 and 6. All of us use our convergent thinking abilities to solve some problems and our divergent thinking abilities to solve others. Sometimes, we use both our divergent and convergent thinking combined with our evaluative skills to decide which of several equally attractive solutions we should implement.

Take today as an example. I (June Maker) have already solved a variety of types of problems. On the 'closed' end of the continuum, I spent a long time finding out what is the ONE appropriate method for extending the visa of a visiting scholar, and began to set in motion a chain of events that would result in the problem being resolved in the only way possible. On the 'open' end of the continuum, I started to write an article. I had only been given a list of general requirements: the title needed to be the same as the one I submitted for the conference ('Creativity, problem-solving, multiple intelligences, and diversity'); it needed to have from 13,000 to 15,000 characters; it needed to have certain basic components such as an introduction, the problem approach, results, conclusion, and recommendations; it could be research-based or practical; and it would be published in a book entitled *Diversity Appreciation and Education*. To solve this problem, I not only drew from my knowledge and past experience, but I also used my divergent thinking and creative thinking skills to present my research and practice in a new way and from another angle so I wouldn't repeat significant parts of previous publications. I had to evaluate my creative ideas and edit my writing to ensure that the final form accommodated the criteria I was given and met my personal standards of quality. I must admit that I found this open-ended problem situation much more fun and fulfilling than finding out the appropriate method (and applying it) to solve the visa extension problem. However, both types were equally challenging!

We believe strongly that all types of problem-solving situations should be included in the curriculum. Unfortunately, too much of education is focused on presenting, solving, and evaluating solutions to Type 1 and Type 2 problems and fails to give pupils opportunities to struggle with the more open-ended types of problems that will be a significant part of their career experiences. In an assessment situation, all types of problem-solving situations are appropriate, but again, unfortunately, too often the assessment contains only Problem Types 1 and 2, which serve the purpose of identifying whether the pupils know and can apply *particular* information instead of finding out *what* information the pupils know and *how* they can use that information purposefully – a goal that can be achieved by using Problem Types 3 to 6.

Reflecting on and extending the theory and practice of DISCOVER

June Maker and Shirley Schiever began their research and development of the principles and practices that have become known as DISCOVER in 1987. Since then, many colleagues have contributed to this work, and we have received funding from various agencies in the US Department of Education and from the Navajo Indian Nation. We developed a performance-based assessment of problem-solving in spatial artistic, spatial analytical, logical-mathematical, oral linguistic, written linguistic, interpersonal, and intrapersonal intelligences, and have conducted numerous studies of its reliability and validity. Working with many teachers from varied cultural backgrounds, languages, and from several countries (including countries vastly different from each other, such as Mainland China and England), we have sought to develop and implement the problem-solving continuum across the multiple intelligences identified by Gardner. In several studies, we examined the effects of using this kind of curriculum on both creativity and achievement. The results of this research and development are summarised in an article in *Gifted Education International* (Maker 2001).

The purposes of the present book are to build on this research, to revisit Gardner's theory, and to integrate DISCOVER with TASC in order to create an exciting new framework for viewing human abilities and fresh ways to apply the problem continuum described in this chapter. The key principles we outlined in Chapter 1 provide the scaffold for this integration of ideas. Let's revisit those principles to see how they relate to problem-solving using the six problem types described in this chapter.

1. The development of vital general learning capacities

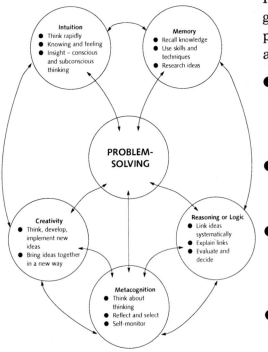

Referring to Mindmap 2 (p. 5), in which the vital general learning capacities are outlined, DISCOVER provides many opportunities for using, developing and improving:

● *Memory* – as pupils recall methods they have been taught, information they have learned about a problem situation, and solutions that have been tried;

● *Intuition* – as teachers allow pupils to have 'aha!' experiences and rely on their inner guidance in defining and solving problems;

● *Creative thinking* – as teachers encourage learners to think of different methods and unique solutions or to apply information they have learned in new and different ways;

● *Reasoning and logic* – as teachers ask learners to meet a clearly defined objective and apply what they have learned, and as pupils are encouraged to develop criteria and evaluate the effectiveness of their own methods and solutions;

● *Metacognition* – as teachers ask pupils to reflect on the effectiveness of their methods and solutions, and give children guidance in choosing and defining problems of interest to them.

2. Using the full range of human abilities

Considering the full range of human abilities outlined in Mindmap 3 (pp. 14–15), DISCOVER is easy to apply to each human ability and can be used to combine and integrate these abilities. Mindmaps 14 and 15 provide examples of how each problem type can be designed to give pupils opportunities to exercise each of their abilities.

3. *Developing learning processes*

Mindmap 4 (p. 16) encapsulates the wide range of learning processes that need to be developed, and the DISCOVER Framework allows and encourages pupils to use all these processes and more. For example, when solving a Type 1 problem, pupils may *decode* the written description of the problem, *listen* while the teacher explains a new method, and then *remember* how to reach a solution. While working on a Type 4 problem, one pupil might *imagine* how to make a new toy, another might *compose* a song, another might *invent* a robot, and still another might *transform* the classroom into a television studio and *record* interviews for a show.

4. *Developing competencies or outcomes*

We need to ask ourselves what competencies and understandings children will need to enable them to function effectively in their world of tomorrow and find ways to integrate rather than separate these important outcomes (see Mindmap 6 on p. 19). The teachers who have contributed to the development of curricula using DISCOVER/TASC have shown time and again that certain universal themes are present across all content areas and even across the national standards and curricula of varied and diverse nations. In Mindmap 14 (p. 66) the general theme is 'Children's Play' and it provides examples of how this theme can be developed through the National Curriculum for Key Stage 1. The general theme of Mindmap 15 (p. 68) is 'Ancient Culture' and this provides examples of how this theme can be developed through the National Curriculum at Key Stage 2.

Conclusion

In the first three chapters we have discussed the principles that underlie both TASC and DISCOVER, and we have suggested that it is indeed possible to work within the National Curriculum Framework while extending and tweaking lesson planning to accommodate problem-solving *processes* and a range of problem *types* across the full range of human abilities. It is now necessary to examine the practical classroom grassroots implementation of these principles in two schools. Chapter 4 outlines in detail a long-term action research programme which has put the principles of DISCOVER/TASC into action over a period of four years. Chapter 5 outlines another action research programme, implemented over a shorter period, for those schools who might consider starting a DISCOVER/TASC whole-school development programme.

Developing an Inclusive School Policy with Differentiation

Using the TASC Problem-solving Process and DISCOVER problem types to raise motivation and achievement across the full range of multiple abilities

DIANA CAVE

Every child begins life with powerful potential light just waiting to be switched on into the smiling glow of achievement: and as teachers, our deep and lasting professional satisfaction comes from our experiences of seeing children manifesting this latent potential through a wide range of abilities. The greatest gifts we can give the children in our care are the skills of learning how to learn and perform with joy, independence and autonomy. How can we ever know how many hearts and minds we have touched forever, and how much of ourselves is stored in the memories of the thousands of children who pass through our classrooms?

(Belle Wallace)

This chapter describes a whole-school approach to the development of thinking and problem-solving across the full range of human abilities. The development has taken three years with each incremental phase of development taking place throughout one academic year.

All the photographs and examples of children's work used in this chapter are from the National CE Junior School, Grantham, Lincs.

Summary of Phase 1: Developing TASC across the curriculum

In Phase 1, following a Training Day, the school decided to adopt the TASC Approach to the development of problem-solving and thinking skills. We trialled the TASC Framework firstly through a series of small pilot studies in a number of areas of the school curriculum, then we shared this work with the whole staff. The staff decided to extend the TASC Approach through dedicating a whole week to introduce the children to TASC through an exciting practical project based on developing class rules and creating TASC advertising slogans, posters and artefacts.

This was followed with staff transferring the TASC Framework and the teaching and learning principles and methods into a number of curriculum areas:

● The Year 3 curriculum team opted to plan all science lessons using the TASC Model.

● The Year 4 team decided to plan and implement TASC in history with a project on Ancient Egypt.

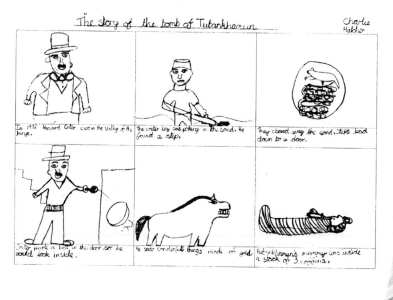

● Year 5 teachers also decided to develop a TASC technology project.

● The Year 6 curriculum team chose to look at aspects of Literacy and Numeracy and tried to decide when and how they could embed the TASC Approach.

Much of this development which we see as Phase 1 has been written up in detail in Wallace (2001; 2003).

Summary of Phase 2: Developing TASC and DISCOVER across the curriculum

In Phase 2, we decided to continue with our TASC Approach, but to reflect on our planning and decide whether we were incorporating lesson activities that gave children adequate opportunities to express their ideas across the full range of multiple abilities. We also decided to examine our planning to analyse whether we were using a range of learning activities that allowed children to investigate problems that ranged from closed to open-ended. The TASC Framework provides a coherent framework for whole-school development of the *universal processes* of thinking and problem-solving; and the DISCOVER Framework provides the rationale for analysing *types* of problem across the range of *multiple abilities*.

Summary of Phase 3: Consolidating and extending DISCOVER/TASC across the multiple abilities

After reflecting on the outcomes of Phase 2, we decided to extend and refine our work further with regard to greater recognition and the diagnostic assessment of pupils' multiple abilities. We also decided to tweak our lesson planning further to make sure that we were accommodating the TASC Problem-solving Process, and the full range of DISCOVER problem types across the multiple abilities.

Phases 2 and 3 are discussed in further detail below.

Phase 2: Developing TASC and DISCOVER across the curriculum

Through working with TASC, staff had become gradually more aware of the multiple abilities. We noted with great interest which abilities we had incorporated into our TASC history project and those which we had not included (see Wallace 2003).

I attended a training day run by June Maker which introduced me to the 'DISCOVER' Project, in which strong links are made between the multiple abilities and problem types, ranging from closed to open-ended. I gathered further information from the 'DISCOVER' website (see 'Websites of interest' at the back of the book), and after reporting back to staff, we decided to focus the attention of the next TASC Week as usual on a series of open-ended activities, but now making certain that we incorporated the full range of multiple abilities.

So, in preparation for this, all staff completed questionnaires (see Appendix 1C, Checklist 2) which encouraged us to discuss and reflect on our own range of multiple abilities and preferred learning modes and activities. As a consequence, our own awareness and understanding of the multiple abilities increased dramatically. We affirmed our individual strengths and became more conscious of our less favoured learning and teaching modes. The whole staff was deeply engaged in this discussion and, consequently, we examined our lesson planning looking to see the quality and breadth of the learning opportunities that we offered children across the multiple abilities.

The children were also encouraged to explore their preferred learning modes. For Years 3 and 4, we gathered together photographs taken during lessons and organised them onto A3 sheets in collages that reflected a range of activities within each of the multiple abilities.

We asked the children to discuss the photograph collages drawn from their lessons and to put the A3 sheets in order of their personal preferences. This was a rewarding opportunity to talk to each child informally about their strengths and weaknesses at the beginning of a new school year. The children then recorded their personal profile onto their name cards for future reference.

My preferred learning activities by								
Human ability	**PSHE**	**Linguistic**	**Mathematical**	**Scientific**	**Mechanical**	**Artistic**	**Musical**	**Movement**
Activity	Circle time discussion about the school community.	Writing a letter for the school magazine.	Designing and making a number game.	Testing the best design for a boat.	Designing and making a mechanism to deliver a conker.	Designing a fun place for the community to relax in.	Creating music to tell the story of Noah's Ark.	Creating and performing a dance based on animal movements.
Preferred order								

The pupils in Years 5 and 6 completed a multiple intelligence questionnaire (see Appendix 1C, Checklist 1), exploring and discussing, in pairs or small groups, each statement in turn, and finally reflecting on their individual preferences for activities and modes of learning.

The children in all years were completely engaged and motivated to discuss the range of learning modes they preferred and enjoyed. Staff compiled a class summary of preferred learning modes, noting particular trends in their own classes.

Our next step was to look at multiple abilities in relation to the categories of problem types. Staff were encouraged to audit the weekly planning of the range of activities they had prepared for the children. They were surprised, and rather taken aback to realise that:

● firstly, they were not regularly including opportunities for open-ended problem-solving; and,

● secondly, they were focusing most of the children's learning activities around Linguistic ability presented in written mode.

This was in conflict with the revelations provided by the children's analysis of their preferred learning modes in which the more practical, hands-on activities across the full range of abilities proved most popular.

After much discussion, we decided that focusing on the snapshot of a weekly plan was rather misleading. We considered that a half-termly audit would be a more accurate measure, since it would include the more open-ended activities which followed after a range of skills had been taught and practised: for example, children did engage in open-ended problem-solving in design technology, but only after they had been taught a range of key skills. In addition, in science it had been necessary to make sure that the children had the understanding and practical experience of using electrical circuits, insulators and conductors before they could tackle the more open-ended problem of designing and making a lamp for a particular purpose which they identified.

Planning Sheets 1–4 show how we tried to plan so that we incorporated activities across the full range of problem types and multiple abilities. In all activities, we used the TASC Approach as far as it was applicable: for example, we sometimes referred to the whole problem-solving TASC Wheel, or to relevant segments as the lesson gave opportunities. It is important to say at this point that we also planned lessons in which the children learned a new skill, or practised a known routine or collection of routines.

Planning for the ten multiple abilities, learning modes and activities
PLANNING SHEET 1

June Y4	Type 1: Clearly defined; Known method; Correct answer	Type 2: Clearly defined; Select method; Correct answer	Type 3: Clearly defined; Create method; Correct answer	Type 4: Clearly defined; Create method; Best answer; Specified criteria	Type 5: Clearly defined; Unknown method; Best answer; Own criteria	Type 6: Not clearly defined; Unknown method; Best answer; Own criteria
1 Social	With your partner, decide on questions and answers posed by the branching key.		What goes into my body? Discuss. Group responses into different categories.		*Explain in words, pictures or drama what happens when our bodies have too much of something.*	
2 / 3 Emotional/Spiritual	Identify the Five pillars of Islam and the significance they hold for Muslims.		Write a diary entry about the visit to the zoo.		Design a mindmap to show all the things you think you have to keep safe from.	
4 Linguistic/Verbal (Set 1)	Spelling test and dictation. Collect compound words.	Explain when each type of written presentational skill is used.	Write a report of the services available in each of the settlements seen in the video 'Village, Town and City'.	Evaluate advertisements for their impact, appeal and honesty. Summarise a paragraph by identifying the most important elements and rewording briefly.	*Identify and discuss social and moral issues in 'Bill's New Frock'.*	Invent a product and persuade people to buy it.
5 Mathematical (Set 3)	Develop and refine written methods for TU x U. Identify multiples of numbers.	Solve problems involving multiplication.	Order containers based on their estimated volume. Check and record volumes.			
6 Scientific	Use a branching key to sort a set of minibeasts.		Use reference books to research and record food chains. Which is the longest food chain you can find?		Devise your own branching key to sort a set of animals.	
7 Mechanical/Technical		Attach textured lid to Isabella box base. Use wooden strips and the toolbox to build an Isabella box.				
8 Visual/Spatial			Compare the eighteenth- and twentieth-century maps of Grantham.	Experiment with a range of pencils to copy the textures that they can see and feel.	Add colour to the textured lid of an Isabella box.	*Explore papier-mâché, modroc, fabric, string, textured gels, pasta and seeds in creating textures.*
9 Auditory/Musical	Listen to music in assembly and join in with the daily hymn. Name the family each instrument comes from.	Add percussion to a calypso rhythm.				*Compose a short piece of music on keyboards as a background to a cartoon.*
10 Movement	In pairs, practise throwing (underarm and overarm) and catching (two hands, one hand, other hand) small balls.	Play small-sided games of rounders.	Find pathways at different levels across the hall, travelling in a variety of ways – with different body parts leading.	Using what you already know about the rules and the skills used in cricket, make up your own version of the game.		

Planning for the ten multiple abilities, learning modes and activities
PLANNING SHEET 2

2 Sept Y4	Type 1: Clearly defined; Known method; Correct answer	Type 2: Clearly defined; Select method; Correct answer	Type 3: Clearly defined; Create method; Correct answer	Type 4: Clearly defined; Create method; Best answer; Specified criteria	Type 5: Clearly defined; Unknown method; Best answer; Own criteria	Type 6: Not clearly defined; Unknown method; Best answer; Own criteria
1 Social		Draw straight and curved lines for your partner to measure using a range of instruments.		In a group, discuss elements of daily life that would have been made easy/difficult by the Egyptian landscape. Work in 2s or 3s to create a dance sequence to a given piece of music.		
2 3 Emotional/ Spiritual	Look at artefacts used in church and school worship. Identify their purpose.					Reflect on and express ideas for the theme 'Being a Team Member' for our class assembly. Consider the character of God.
4 Linguistic/ Verbal	Spelling test and dictation. Identify basic verbs in sentences. Use spell check to correct mistakes.	Suggest replacements to basic verbs in sentences. Rewrite instructions changing verbs from present to past tense.	Look at a list of words that can be both verbs and nouns. Suggest sentences that show the difference between them.	Write brief planning notes for a new story as a sequel to 'The Glass Cupboard'. Write a character sketch of one of the characters from the class story.	Identify and develop the settings of some very brief fiction extracts.	Explore how you could produce your own character sketch.
5 Mathematical	Name shapes. Introduce 'perimeter'. Measure lengths and calculate perimeters of different shapes.	Show children how to use metre sticks to measure a length which is longer than I m. Record I m 36 cm. Discuss 136 cm and I.36 m. Repeat for other objects, estimating first.	Display a 30 cm ruler, metre stick, trundle wheel and tape measure. Discuss 'What would you use to measure…?' Explain choice. Estimate and measure a variety of lengths.			
6 Scientific	Illustrate and explain the 'Water Cycle'.	Construct electrical circuits. Investigate materials and sort into 'conductors' and 'insulators'.	Find a fault in a simple circuit and correct it.	Create a model of 'The Iron Man' in which his eyes flash on and off. Evaluate a variety of switches and write a 'Which Switch?' review.	Produce a mind map to show all that is known about electricity.	
7 Mechanical/ Technical	Identify the key features of a torch and explain how a torch works.			Investigate a collection of torches and make observations.	Design a new type of battery operated lamp which satisfies certain needs of the person who will use it.	
8 Visual/Spatial	Watch BBC video 'Rivers'. Make observations and answer questions. Identify river features on a map. Revise work on primary and secondary colours.	Draw a simple timeline to show the events, the passage of time and the structure of the story.	Look at illustrations in class storybook. Analyse how the images have been sequenced in relation to the story.	Discuss how stories have been represented visually e.g. Egyptian tomb paintings, Greek vases, Chinese ceramics, Bayeux Tapestry.	Investigate and use a range of materials and techniques to create surface patterns and other visual techniques.	
9 Musical/ Auditory	Sing hymns in assembly. Listen to a variety of music. Identify different kinds of rhythm and beat.	Explore similarities and differences between percussion instruments that are struck. Explore instruments from other countries.		Add accompaniment to 'Nervous Knight' using junk materials.		Create a sound story based on 'The Nervous Knight'.
10 Movement	Locate Egypt and the Nile on a globe and in atlases. Warming up activities for dance.	Estimate and measure classroom objects with ¹⁄₂ ¹⁄₄ ³⁄₄ metre strips. Revise pushing and receiving, striking and receiving a ball.		Develop ball control by dribbling a ball in a set area without making contact with others. Introduce interception of passes. Play 2 v I.	Respond to music and poetry: paired travelling sequence developing rhythmic phrasing: solo phrase with contrasting dynamics; pupils develop group dance.	Respond to music to develop dance sequences.

© Diana Cave, Belle Wallace and June Maker (2004) *Thinking Skills and Problem-Solving – An Inclusive Approach*, David Fulton Publishers.

Planning for the ten multiple abilities, learning modes and activities
PLANNING SHEET 3

3 March Y4	Type 1: Clearly defined; Known method; Correct answer	Type 2: Clearly defined; Select method; Correct answer	Type 3: Clearly defined; Create method; Correct answer	Type 4: Clearly defined; Create method; Best answer; Specified criteria	Type 5: Clearly defined; Unknown method; Best answer; Own criteria	Type 6: Not clearly defined; Unknown method; Best answer; Own criteria
1 Social				As s group, prepare a dramatic reading of 'Jabberwocky' to present to the rest of the class.		
2 3 Emotional/ Spiritual			Draw and label foods which they should eat more often and those which should be eaten less often.	Take notes while listening to a story and rewrite the notes as a diary entry. Discuss whose responsibility it is to keep us healthy.	Use role play to re-enact Jesus' entry into Jerusalem on Palm Sunday. Decide what should be done about pollution. Write a letter to the editor of the local newspaper.	*Explain what it is like to be in an excited crowd.* *Communicate how it feels to lose someone or something special.*
4 Linguistic/ Verbal (Set 1)	Spelling test and dictation. Recognise a range of suffixes.	Discuss how language changes over time. Read 'The Listeners'. What makes the poem seem old. Collect words and phrases from poems and assemble a word bank of examples.		Predict the end of the story 'Fair's Fair'. Fill in the gaps in a limerick to complete the rhyming pattern, then write a new limerick.	Write a nonsense verse modelled on 'Jabberwocky'. Make a poster to show ways in which poetry is different from prose.	*Use words to describe a river.*
5 Mathematical (Set 3)	Practise speedy recall of 10 times table facts. Read the time from an analogue clock to the nearest minute and from a 12-hour digital clock. Use a.m. and p.m. and the notation 9:53.	Use thermometers to measure the temperatures of different beakers of water. Use a stopwatch to measure the speed of the river's flow.	Use informal pencil and paper methods to explain multiplication and division. Choose and use appropriate number operations to solve problems.			
6 Scientific		Compare samples of river water, bottled water and tap water. Discuss differences in colour and clarity.	Explore and describe how powders and solids consisting of very small particles behave like liquids.	Classify and label a variety of materials.	Suggest ways of categorising foods. Explore what happens when a range of materials are mixed with water; group the solids according to what happens.	
7 Mechanical/ Technical	Explore instructions needed for a floor turtle to draw a square. Introduce the concept of a repeat loop.	Write a program using Logo to draw your initials on screen.	Program Roamer to complete an obstacle course designed by a partner.			
8 Visual/Spatial	Practise handwriting patterns. View the OHTs of part of the River Witham identifying examples of pollution.		Draw a flowchart to show how water reaches our homes.	Design an image for a child's alphabet frieze using fabric crayons. Produce an appliqué letter using a variety of fabrics and threads.		*Create a product to advertise 'The Lion, the Witch and the Wardrobe'.*
9 Auditory/ Musical	Sing hymns in assembly. Listen to a variety of music. Identify rhythm and beat.	Create a whole-class musical performance based on 'Jelly on a plate'. Rehearse in 3 groups using untuned percussion. Concentrate on the pulse and rhythm.	Listen to 'Noye's Fludde' by Britten. Discuss the use of different voices for Noah, the children and the animals. Describe what is happening in the extract.			
10 Movement	Warming up activity for PE. Revise pushing and receiving/ striking and receiving a ball.		Develop ball control by dribbling a ball in a set area without making contact with others. Introduce idea of attack and defence. Play hockey 3 v 3.		With 3 different ways of balancing, change smoothly from one to the next. Refine actions and body control. Link movements to establish a simple gymnastic sequence.	

Planning for the ten multiple abilities, learning modes and activities
PLANNING SHEET 4

4 April Y4	Type 1: Clearly defined; Known method; Correct answer	Type 2: Clearly defined; Select method; Correct answer	Type 3: Clearly defined; Create method; Correct answer	Type 4: Clearly defined; Create method; Best answer; Specified criteria	Type 5: Clearly defined; Unknown method; Best answer; Own criteria	Type 6: Not clearly defined; Unknown method; Best answer; Own criteria
1 Social				In groups, make up your own country dance.	Work together in ICT to produce a flower pattern using Logo.	Consider the things people say when they are persuading others to do something they don't want to do. Explore unapologetic/assertive ways of answering persuasive people.
2 3 Emotional/ Spiritual				Evaluate your finished textile panel against the design criteria you set. Does it meet those requirements? How could it be better? What would you change?	Consider Jesus' feelings on the night of the Last Supper. Write a diary entry. Consider 'Who owns water?'	
4 Linguistic/ Verbal (Set 1)	Spelling test and dictation. Answer questions about the extract from 'Boy'.	Write a short comparison of the extracts from 'Matilda' and 'Boy'. Examine how short sentences make the incident in 'The Magic Finger' quite tense.	Read extract from 'Matilda'. Summarise similarities between Matilda and Dahl's practical joke in 'The Great Mouse Plot'.	Discuss text and term 'biography'. Read and discuss extract from 'Boy' and term 'autobiography'. What do they learn about Dahl?	Discuss work of Roald Dahl. Discuss characters and funny or exciting parts of his stories. What did they like or dislike about them? Make a chart.	Use words to promote your favourite Roald Dahl book.
5 Mathematical (Set 3)	Recognise simple fractions that are several parts of a whole. Find doubles and halves of given numbers.	Recognise equivalence of simple fractions. Recognise the equivalence between the decimal and fraction forms of the tenths.	Solve a given problem by collecting, classifying, representing and interpreting data in bar charts.			
6 Scientific			Discuss ways of separating a mixture of solids. Decide on the best method. Choose apparatus to separate an undissolved solid from a liquid.			
7 Mechanical/ Technical	Follow Logo instructions using repeat sequences.	Predict what will appear on screen after entering a given Logo sequence. Test hypotheses.			Use repeat procedures on Logo to produce a flower pattern.	
8 Visual/ Spatial	Practise handwriting patterns.				Design a poster advertising your favourite Roald Dahl book.	Create a textile panel for an alphabet frieze.
9 Musical/ Auditory	Sing hymns in assembly. Listen to a variety of music, identifying rhythm and beat.		Listen to music. Discuss the voices for Noah, children and animals. Describe what is happening in the story extract.			
10 Movement		Perform a country dance to music.	Develop ball control by dribbling a ball in a set area without making contact with others. Introduce idea of attack and defence. Play hockey 3 v 3.	Using the movements learned, make up your own country dance to music.		Display your reaction to music by moving freely.

Reflection on Phase 2

- As a staff we were now used to using the TASC Framework in lessons, and the children became more familiar and confident in referring to the TASC Wheel to structure their thinking and problem-solving. Our more able children could use the TASC Wheel confidently to structure their own projects and enquiry, and it was easier to set differentiated and independent work that required greater depth and breadth. We observed that our more able children were identifying for themselves which aspects of the TASC Wheel they needed to use at any stage in their thinking, and they were confidently transferring the problem-solving processes across the curriculum. They were able to take greater ownership of their learning, and became increasingly independent learners; however, in the TASC stage of gathering and organising what they already knew, and in the final presentation and communication of work, we were keen to work in an inclusive way with the whole class. The less able children could use the TASC Framework as a crutch to scaffold and break down their thinking processes into stages. They needed more help and structured support, but they were using the TASC Problem-solving Wheel to help in their planning especially in the more open-ended activities.

- As a staff we were more keenly aware of our forward planning in that we tried to build in a range of problem types, and to incorporate opportunities for the children to use the full range of multiple abilities. We were far more understanding of the children who had abilities outside the Linguistic, Mathematical and Scientific abilities. We scrutinised the wording of our questions, since the wording could change the type of problem we presented. We tried, as often as possible, to allow the children to present their work through a range of their preferred learning modes, but we were also aware of their need to work across all the multiple abilities – finding great satisfaction in using their strengths, but also developing those abilities which were their less dominant ones.

- We realised that there is a definite need for problem-solving across the closed Types 1 and 2, but we were more aware of the need to include the more creative, open-ended types of problem-solving across all subjects. There is obviously a clear difference between Type 1 and Type 6 problem-solving activities, but the boundaries between Types 3 and 4 are blurred, and also the same applies to Types 5 and 6. However, although the problem types form a continuum with blurred boundaries, the purpose of delineating the six types is to clarify our thinking when we are planning activities for children. Usually, it is in the clarification of the *wording* of the task that the problem *type* is revealed.

● As a staff we became far more aware of the range of recording skills we were developing with the children, and we were more careful to display the children's stages of thinking – putting up our displays of work around the TASC Wheel.

● We communicated and celebrated what we were achieving through displays and productions for parents and governors, and we set up an exhibition in the local library.

Phase 3: Consolidating and extending DISCOVER/TASC across the multiple abilities

We envisaged TASC Week 2003 as being even more exciting than in the past. Previously, we had used TASC Week to develop class activities around a theme. Now we decided to use the TASC Framework to offer the children the opportunity to explore and reflect on their preferred learning modes and abilities in a very practical way. Previously, we had used questionnaires and photo montages drawn from actual lessons as the basis for these discussions and reflections. But this year we decided to make the exploration even more practical and more systematic – along the lines of June Maker's DISCOVER Model.

We initially felt that the prospect of planning and carrying out this task was daunting, since we knew that the DISCOVER activities are carried out with the help of several university master students supporting each group leader in the investigation of just one human ability.[1] However, because of the size of our school (16 classes), we allocated five days for the project and accepted the challenge. We also accepted the challenge that each member of staff would develop all the activities with her or his class so that she or he would gather together a profile of the whole class across the full range of human abilities.

Some members of staff were instantly a little concerned as the 'normal' timetable would be 'switched off' and there would be hardly any specialist teaching of music etc. Other members of staff were anxious that such a highly practical week at the start of a new school year would make it difficult to re-establish standards of work and acceptable behaviour after the long summer break. With these concerns in mind, we planned for TASC Week to occur in the week before the autumn half-term break. By this

---

1 June Maker has developed a training programme for teachers in the Assessment of Human Abilities, but it has not been possible, as yet, to run this training course in the UK.

time, staff felt they would be familiar with their children, and that high standards of both work and behaviour would be the norm.

So, we began the planning. The TASC Framework was used as a matter of course since staff were now familiar with using it, and confident in working with it across the whole curriculum.

Starting information was **gathered and organised**. First of all, we considered whether we would design activities across all the abilities. We decided to prepare highly practical activities for each of the Linguistic, Mathematical, Scientific, Mechanical/ Technical, Visual/Spatial, Auditory and Movement abilities; and we would prepare one activity combining the Social, Emotional and Spiritual abilities into one PSHE task.

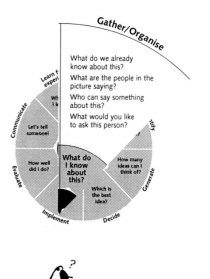

We also decided to invite parents into school to support activities where extra hands would be most useful. Lacking in both experience and student support, we realised that it would be impossible to achieve the high level of monitoring and assessment which is a key feature of DISCOVER. Nevertheless, it would be possible to gain a *snapshot* of the children's abilities, identifying those children whose commitment and achievement was beyond our expectations, and those where greater than anticipated support was needed. We agreed that we would extend and possibly change this initial snapshot as we worked with the children throughout the year, and noted their growth and development.

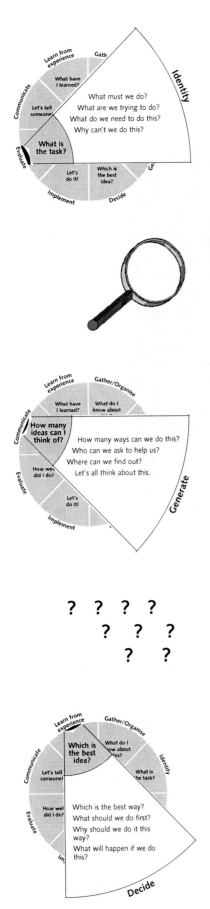

As a staff, we use the TASC Framework for our own planning, so we focused our attention on *identifying the task* – this was to decide on a general theme and then on the specifics of each of the activities. We had a clear intention of keeping the management of the week as tight as possible while creating opportunities for the children to work in open-ended and creative ways.

As the Gifted and Talented Coordinator, I was responsible for the organisation of TASC Week in consultation with the Head teacher, John Gibbs, and Belle Wallace. I met with curriculum leaders to agree on the timing of TASC Week and on a theme for the week. Early ideas had been on the theme of 'New Beginnings', but now that our TASC Week had been moved six weeks into the term, it no longer seemed appropriate. Suggestions were made for links with 'Belonging' – the children all belonged to new classes and year groups and, of course, one quarter of the children were new to the school. The 'Healthy Schools' initiative is also a high priority in the school. We eventually settled on the theme of 'Community' for our TASC Week, since we believe that strengthening the Social, Emotional and Spiritual abilities of all children gives them a firm base for their future growth and development.

The next step was to *generate* ideas. In curriculum teams, which had a representative from each year group, we eagerly discussed possible activities. We had already decided that, where possible, we would develop a single activity for each human ability. Each activity could then be adapted for each year group and differentiated as appropriate. The activities were to be as open-ended as possible to allow children to think freely and show their capabilities. We suggested approximate timings for each activity, and drew up lists of resources. These were important considerations and the week needed to be carefully organised: each activity would vary in length – some activities needing whole mornings or afternoons, and some resources, such as the musical instruments and the use of the school hall, would need to be shared on a rota basis.

Then it was time to *decide*. Belle Wallace and I met with each subject leader to evaluate ideas, select the most suitable one and draft a lesson plan. Staff enthusiasm and previous experience of using the TASC Framework enabled subject leaders to come to these meetings with a good idea of how each activity would develop. However, a major problem with the Mechanical/Technical ability plan arose at this time. The DT team had met and discussed ideas relating to the challenge of transporting an object from one community to another using construction kits. But the resources in school were either not appropriate or of insufficient quantity for all four years to use. So, the challenge for each year group was adapted and separated: Year 3 were to use card, paper and tape; Year 4 card, paper, tape, string and pulleys; Year 5 'Kinex'; and Year 6 'Inventa'.

We then held a whole-school staff meeting at which all lesson plans were presented to staff. Each subject leader introduced and explained their particular plan and staff discussed each one. Some staff felt apprehension as they were expected to work in ability areas that were not their particular strengths. The Auditory/Musical and Mechanical/Technical activities seemed to conjure up the most anxiety from a few members of staff, and I emphasised that support would be available. I tried to give plenty of encouragement as we discussed all concerns, and a few 'swaps' were negotiated. Subject leaders promised to make themselves available for further consultation.

The few lingering worries over the lesson plans for the activities were discussed in year group meetings, and final tweaking to differentiate the tasks was carried out. The deployment of Learning Support Assistants was negotiated and timetables were drawn up to accommodate the demand on limited resources. We decided to carry out the Linguistic and Mathematical activities in the children's usual Literacy and Numeracy sets which are organised on the basis of ability. All other activities would take place in mixed-ability class groups.

Belle Wallace and I discussed the monitoring and evaluation that was to be conducted during TASC Week. Staff were asked to make detailed notes relating to each segment of the TASC Wheel, noting, in particular, those children whose contribution was greater than normal. We also compiled an evaluation sheet for the children which was to be completed at the end of the week. These suggestions were also shared and discussed with staff.

So, all plans had been shared: the staff expressed their feelings of genuine ownership of the planning and decision-making; and apart from a little anticipatory nervousness, everyone was happy and looking forward to what we knew would be an action-packed week!

Planning Sheets 5–12 (pp. 90–7) summarise the organisation agreed on by the staff.

TASC Week arrived. It was time to ***implement*** the planning. The assembly theme for the week reflected the TASC Week title of 'Community' and we got off to an exciting start. There was a constant buzz around the school. Everyone was smiling! Fewer children seemed to get into trouble, either in class or on the playground.

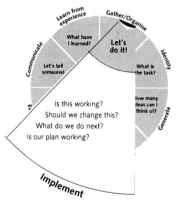

PLANNING SHEET 5

	Date	Curriculum Area	**Linguistic ability**	Cross-curricular/ **PSHE links**

PSHE 1a 4a – explain views on issues

POS	**Learning Objective:** **To write a non-chronological letter from known information and to articulate responses to the letter.**

Introduction:
Gather/Organise: What do I already know about this?
Generate: How many ideas can I think of?
Year 3. What do you remember most about your first week at the National School?
Years 4 to 6. What are the most enjoyable things at the National School?
Produce concept maps – memories; feelings; reasons for writing.

Vocabulary
Dear
Yours sincerely
Yours faithfully

Activity:
Identify: What is the task?
Examine letters pages from newspapers and magazines.
Note that the school newspaper doesn't contain a letters page.
We will be looking for letters to include in the school newspaper.
Choose one thing that stands out to produce a newsletter contribution.
Specify the criteria for evaluation: how will I know if it's a good letter?

Differentiation
By task, by outcome, by teacher/LSA input

Support

Decide: Which is the best idea? Implement: Let's do it!
Select ideas and words from concept maps and write a short letter to the editor.

Evaluate: How well did I do? Communicate: Let's tell someone!
Distribute letters for editorial reading.
Each group to read a number of letters and to select and present one letter explaining why they have decided to included this letter in the school bulletin.

Resources
Children's magazines with letters pages
Newspapers

Plenary:
Learn from experience: What have I learned?
What have I learned from the letters about the experiences of others?
What have I learned about writing letters?
What have I learned about working as a member of an editorial team?
What have I learned about my feelings and the feelings of others?
Consider: how would you greet newcomers coming into the school?

Key Assessment

Notes/Implications for future planning:

© Diana Cave, Belle Wallace and June Maker (2004) *Thinking Skills and Problem-Solving – An Inclusive Approach*, David Fulton Publishers.

PLANNING SHEET 6

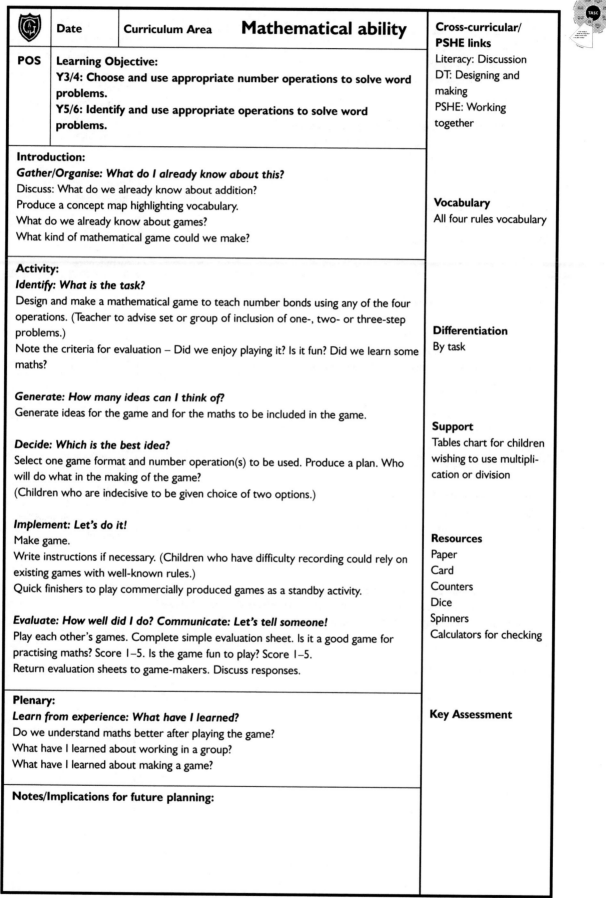

	Date	Curriculum Area	**Mathematical ability**	Cross-curricular/ PSHE links

POS	**Learning Objective:** **Y3/4: Choose and use appropriate number operations to solve word problems.** **Y5/6: Identify and use appropriate operations to solve word problems.**	Literacy: Discussion DT: Designing and making PSHE: Working together

Introduction:
Gather/Organise: What do I already know about this?
Discuss: What do we already know about addition?
Produce a concept map highlighting vocabulary.
What do we already know about games?
What kind of mathematical game could we make?

Vocabulary
All four rules vocabulary

Activity:
Identify: What is the task?
Design and make a mathematical game to teach number bonds using any of the four operations. (Teacher to advise set or group of inclusion of one-, two- or three-step problems.)
Note the criteria for evaluation – Did we enjoy playing it? Is it fun? Did we learn some maths?

Differentiation
By task

Generate: How many ideas can I think of?
Generate ideas for the game and for the maths to be included in the game.

Decide: Which is the best idea?
Select one game format and number operation(s) to be used. Produce a plan. Who will do what in the making of the game?
(Children who are indecisive to be given choice of two options.)

Support
Tables chart for children wishing to use multiplication or division

Implement: Let's do it!
Make game.
Write instructions if necessary. (Children who have difficulty recording could rely on existing games with well-known rules.)
Quick finishers to play commercially produced games as a standby activity.

Resources
Paper
Card
Counters
Dice
Spinners
Calculators for checking

Evaluate: How well did I do? Communicate: Let's tell someone!
Play each other's games. Complete simple evaluation sheet. Is it a good game for practising maths? Score 1–5. Is the game fun to play? Score 1–5.
Return evaluation sheets to game-makers. Discuss responses.

Plenary:
Learn from experience: What have I learned?
Do we understand maths better after playing the game?
What have I learned about working in a group?
What have I learned about making a game?

Key Assessment

Notes/Implications for future planning:

PLANNING SHEET 7

	Date	Curriculum Area	**Scientific ability**	**Cross-curricular/ PSHE links**

Cross-curricular/ PSHE links
English: Discussion
DT: Designing and making
Maths: Measuring mass

POS	**Learning Objective:** To investigate which shape boat will carry the most weight.

Introduction:

Gather/Organise: What do I already know about this?
What do we already know about boats? What shape are they?
What are they used for? How do they move?

Activity:

Identify: What is the task?
Think about boat shapes.
Using one sheet of A4 newspaper, design and make a boat which will carry the most weight.

Generate: How many ideas can I think of?
In groups, discuss how many ways we can make a boat.

Decide: Which is the best idea?
What is the best shape to use?
What is the best way to use the sheet of newspaper?
Each person to make her or his own decision.

Implement: Let's do it!
Make boat 1 and test it.
Evaluate.
Make boat 2, taking into account any problems encountered in boat 1, and test it.

Evaluate: How well did I do? Communicate: Let's tell someone!
Test boats. Record loads next to a class list.
Discuss: Which boat held the most weight? Which shape was best? Why do you think that was?

Plenary:

Learn from experience: What have I learned?
Discuss: What have we learned about making boats? What have we learned about the relationship between weight and shape? What have we learned about working cooperatively?

Notes/Implications for future planning:

Vocabulary
Shape
Force
Upthrust
Streamlined

Differentiation
By outcome

Support
Peer support

Resources
A4 sheets of newsprint
Strips of Sellotape™
Bowls/buckets
10 g masses or marbles, cubes, etc.

Key Assessment

PLANNING SHEET 8

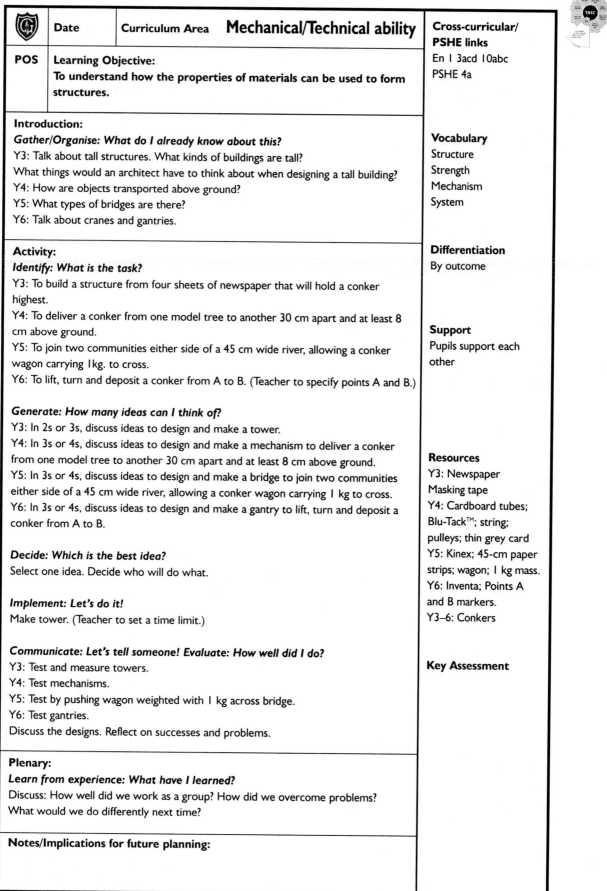

	Date	Curriculum Area	**Mechanical/Technical ability**	**Cross-curricular/ PSHE links**
POS	**Learning Objective:** To understand how the properties of materials can be used to form structures.			En I 3acd 10abc PSHE 4a

Introduction:

Gather/Organise: What do I already know about this?

Y3: Talk about tall structures. What kinds of buildings are tall?

What things would an architect have to think about when designing a tall building?

Y4: How are objects transported above ground?

Y5: What types of bridges are there?

Y6: Talk about cranes and gantries.

Vocabulary
Structure
Strength
Mechanism
System

Activity:

Identify: What is the task?

Y3: To build a structure from four sheets of newspaper that will hold a conker highest.

Y4: To deliver a conker from one model tree to another 30 cm apart and at least 8 cm above ground.

Y5: To join two communities either side of a 45 cm wide river, allowing a conker wagon carrying 1kg. to cross.

Y6: To lift, turn and deposit a conker from A to B. (Teacher to specify points A and B.)

Differentiation
By outcome

Support
Pupils support each other

Generate: How many ideas can I think of?

Y3: In 2s or 3s, discuss ideas to design and make a tower.

Y4: In 3s or 4s, discuss ideas to design and make a mechanism to deliver a conker from one model tree to another 30 cm apart and at least 8 cm above ground.

Y5: In 3s or 4s, discuss ideas to design and make a bridge to join two communities either side of a 45 cm wide river, allowing a conker wagon carrying 1 kg to cross.

Y6: In 3s or 4s, discuss ideas to design and make a gantry to lift, turn and deposit a conker from A to B.

Resources
Y3: Newspaper
Masking tape
Y4: Cardboard tubes;
Blu-Tack™; string;
pulleys; thin grey card
Y5: Kinex; 45-cm paper
strips; wagon; 1 kg mass.
Y6: Inventa; Points A
and B markers.
Y3–6: Conkers

Decide: Which is the best idea?

Select one idea. Decide who will do what.

Implement: Let's do it!

Make tower. (Teacher to set a time limit.)

Communicate: Let's tell someone! Evaluate: How well did I do?

Y3: Test and measure towers.

Y4: Test mechanisms.

Y5: Test by pushing wagon weighted with 1 kg across bridge.

Y6: Test gantries.

Discuss the designs. Reflect on successes and problems.

Key Assessment

Plenary:

Learn from experience: What have I learned?

Discuss: How well did we work as a group? How did we overcome problems? What would we do differently next time?

Notes/Implications for future planning:

PLANNING SHEET 9

	Date	Curriculum Area	**Visual/Spatial ability**	Cross-curricular/ PSHE links
POS	**Learning Objective:** To create a fun place for the community to relax and enjoy themselves.			Art: Communicating ideas English: Discussion Maths: Scale, shape

Introduction:

Gather/Organise: What do I already know about this?

Discuss: Who are the people in our community who need a place to relax and have fun? List all ideas, recording different groups within the community.

Activity:

Identify: What is the task?

Clarify the task.

Which group or groups is the fun place being designed for?

What specific needs do they have?

Generate: How many ideas can I think of?

Individually, or in groups, generate ideas.

What features could be included in their fun place?

How could they represent these features?

Decide: Which is the best idea?

Through writing, drawing or discussing, decide . . .

Which ideas will we include?

Who will do what?

Implement: Let's do it!

Before beginning, discuss constraints of time and resources.

Children to create their fun place.

(Quick finishers could make a detailed enlargement of a specific section of their fun place.)

Evaluate: How well did I do?

Group discussions: How well do we think we have created our fun place?

Is it suitable for the needs of the users?

What was particularly successful?

What mistakes did we make?

Communicate: Let's tell someone!

Present fun places and share evaluations with the class.

Plenary:

Learn from experience: What have I learned?

Discuss: Did we work efficiently as a team?

What have we learned about making plans and models?

Why are plans useful?

What would I do differently next time?

Notes/Implications for future planning:

Cross-curricular/ PSHE links

Art: Communicating ideas
English: Discussion
Maths: Scale, shape
Geography: Local amenities; land use
DT: Design and making
PSHE: Community issues

Vocabulary

Scale
Perspective
Vertical
Horizontal
Shape words

Differentiation

By outcome

Support

LSAs to support named children
Peer support in pairs and groups
Intervention by staff if necessary

Resources

Card
Coloured paper
Planning paper
Glue
Scissors
Crayons, pastels, paint, etc.

Key Assessment

PLANNING SHEET 10

	Date	Curriculum Area	**Auditory/Musical ability**	Cross-curricular/ PSHE links
POS	**Learning Objective:** To create a musical representation of the story of Noah's Ark.			English: Discussion RE: Bible stories PSHE: Working together

Introduction:

Gather/Organise: What do I already know about this?

What do we already know of the story of Noah's Ark?

Produce a flowchart to map sequential events.

Discuss possible 'What if …?' scenarios, e.g. What if the woodpeckers made holes in the ark? What if the cats were in with the mice? etc.

Vocabulary
Sounds
Timbre
Dynamics
Texture, Instruments
Body percussion

Activity:

Identify: What is the task?

Create the story of Noah's Ark ending with a 'What if …?' scenario.

Focus on mood changes – steady procession onto the Ark, rhythms of increasing rain, Noah's voice interjecting, 'What if …?' sounds of conflict or harmony.

Generate: How many ideas can I think of?

Encourage children to discuss and experiment with sounds for each mood/episode, using instruments as well as body percussion to fit their particular sound effect. Conduct demonstrations of unusual sounds.

Differentiation
By outcome

Decide: Which is the best idea?

In groups, decide on instruments/sounds to match actions and animal sounds.

Explain that each group's presentation should be one minute in length.

Support
Mixed-ability groupings

Implement: Let's do it!

Children will be given 10–15 minutes to rehearse their soundtrack.

Halt class after 5 minutes to check for problems.

Resources
Body percussion,
Tuned/non-tuned
percussion

Communicate: Let's tell someone!

Each group to present their oral introduction/explanation followed by soundtrack.

Evaluate: How well did I do?

Did the music portray the events/conflict/harmony of the story?

Which groups were particularly successful?

Key Assessment

Plenary:

Learn from experience: What have I learned?

Discuss: If we were to do it again, how could we improve it?

How do different musical sounds make us feel?

How did we work as a group?

Notes/Implications for future planning:

PLANNING SHEET 11

🛡️	Date	Curriculum Area	**Movement**	Cross-curricular/ PSHE links
				Music 3a 3b
POS	**Learning Objective:** To create and perform a dance showing dynamic and expressive qualities based on animal movements.			English 1 2e 3ab PSHE 4a

Introduction: *Gather/Organise: What do I already know about this?* Play contrasting music from 'The Carnival of the Animals'. Discuss what kinds of animals and movement the music conveys. Produce concept maps for heavy, strong movements and light, flowing movements.	**Vocabulary** Action and reaction Dynamics – weight, space, flow Space – directions, levels, body shape
Activity: *Identify: What is the task?* In groups, create movements to this contrasting music. Prepare a presentation to perform to the rest of the class. *Generate: How many ideas can I think of?* Individually respond to music. Volunteers to demonstrate heavy, strong movements and light, flowing movements. In groups, discuss and practise movements. *Decide: Which is the best idea?* Which movements will we keep and refine? How will we mix them together? Who will perform the heavy, strong movements and who will perform the light, flowing movements? What pose will we freeze and hold when we are not performing? *Implement: Let's do it!* Opportunity to practise to music. Discuss, evaluate and modify performance. Second practice. *Communicate: Let's tell someone! Evaluate: How well did I do?* Each group to perform to the rest of the class. Group evaluation. How well did the movement about the animals communicate? How well did the movement match the music?	**Differentiation** By outcome **Support** Teacher and group support **Resources** Edited tape of 'The Carnival of the Animals' **Key Assessment**
Plenary: *Learn from experience: What have I learned?* How did we work together? How do we feel about moving to music?	
Notes/Implications for future planning:	

PLANNING SHEET 12

	Date	Curriculum Area **Emotional/Social/Spiritual**	**Cross-curricular/ PSHE links**
POS	**Learning Objective:** To know what it means to be a problem-solver in the school community and to understand both sides of an issue.		English: Discussion PSHE: Community issues

Introduction:

Gather/Organise: What do I already know about this?

Circle time: What do we mean by community?

Choose one or two questions from the 'What school means to me' sheet.

Discuss: What are the good and bad things about each situation?

Consider: What do we already know of benefits or problems of situations in school? What other issues are there?

Vocabulary
Community
Responsibility
Sharing

Differentiation
By outcome

Activity:

Identify: What is the task?

In groups, discuss the pros and cons of each issue.

Decide: Which is the best idea?

Decide which one issue to explore.

Decide how to explore it and how to communicate ideas (oral presentation, poster, drama, etc.).

Support
Mixed-ability grouping

Generate: How many ideas can I think of?

Generate ideas based on decisions.

Implement: Let's do it!

Group discussions.

Plan and prepare presentation.

Resources
'What school means to me' sheet

Communicate: Let's tell someone!

Feed back to the rest of the class.

Evaluate: How well did I do?

Return to circle.

Discuss: How well was the point put across?

Key Assessment

Plenary:

Learn from experience: What have I learned?

Discuss: What have I learned about community?

What about situations I find myself in at school? How do I react?

How have we worked as a team?

Notes/Implications for future planning:

Linguistic

Dear Editor,
At the National Junior School we have been talking about our most enjoyable memories. We would like to tell you about our most enjoyable memory. It is Gainsborough Old Hall because we got to dress up in Tudor costumes. We saw the bedrooms which were really grand. The Tudors were quite disgusting and smelly!
Olivia, Leanne, Gemma, Emily and Lara

Tuesday 31.10.03

Dear Editor,
My name is Laura and I go to the National Junior School. I am writing to tell you about one of my wonderful memories at this school. It was when I went to Twycross zoo, a beautiful place with plenty of amusing animals to occupy you and I think it is for all age groups.
The day we went was very appropriate, weather wise, and brilliant fro me because I live animals. I had fun not only because of he animals but because I went with my friends and I know that shows us what a friendly school we are. I am in Year 6 and have had many other fun activities but this was definitely my favourite.

Yours faithfully
Laura.

Recalling happy memories

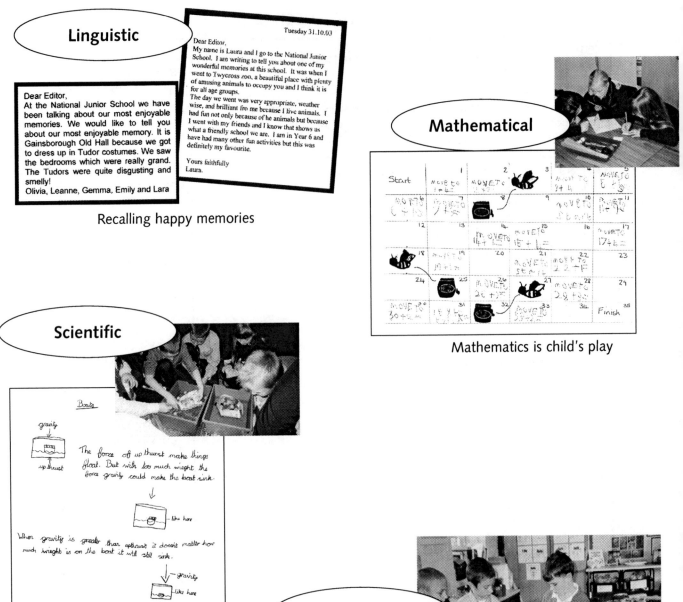

Mathematical

Mathematics is child's play

Scientific

Boats

The force off up thurst make things float. But with too much wieght the force gravity could make the boat sink.

– like here

When gravity is greater than upthrust it doesnt matter how much wieght is on the boat it will still sink.

How many bricks can your boat hold?

Mechanical/Technical

Transport your conkers

Visual/Spatial

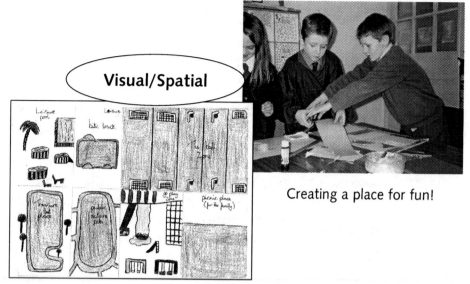

Creating a place for fun!

Movement

Prey or predators

Auditory/Musical

Creating a procession of animal sounds

Social/Emotional and Spiritual

Debating important issues

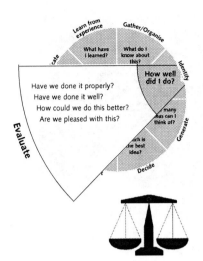

As TASC Week drew to a close, the children were asked to *evaluate* the week and to consider their preferred learning modes and activities. Throughout the week, their enthusiasm and joy had been almost tangible. They had embraced the practical challenges creatively and energetically.

During classroom discussion, the children reminded themselves of the activities they had enjoyed. They talked of their successes and problems, of their admiration for the ingenuity of their classmates, of their pleasure at working with others, and of their delight at not having to write as much as usual. They then completed their evaluation sheets, recording information about their favourite activity, and indicating the order of their preferred learning modes.

Children's comments generally resembled the following:

The staff evaluated each lesson in turn. There had been animated discussion and comparing of notes in the staffroom throughout the whole week. Everyone was tired, but it was a very satisfying tiredness. The week had generated little formal marking and had therefore given staff time to reflect on each lesson more thoroughly. See pages 102–7 for the staff evaluations.

Two parents' evenings took place during TASC Week. Though these were not specifically TASC-oriented, parents and carers were able to view much of the children's work. There were very many comments about the children's enjoyment of the week:

I've heard more about what he's done in the past two days than in the rest of the term.

They can't wait to tell me what they've been doing.

She has been so excited that we have had to repeat all the activities at home.

Designing a maths game inspired her to make another one at home and that has rekindled our interest in playing board games as a family.

Can I come in and see her model playground? She's told me all about it and she's desperate to show me.

He has never been so keen to come to school.

He doesn't usually like dancing, but he enjoyed moving like a lion. He demonstrated all the way home!

In order to **communicate** the success of TASC Week with a wider audience, a display was mounted in the town library. The children were delighted to see their work exhibited where the wider community could view it.

TASC Evaluation

Activity:
Linguistic ability

How did the children respond to each segment of the TASC Wheel?

Gather/Organise and Identify:
It was obvious that few children knew what 'Letters to the Editor' were and so the activity needed explanation and careful structuring. Lower-ability children in all years, together with the younger children, needed help with the letter format, opening sentence, appropriate language.

Generate and Decide:
Most teachers worked as a class to generate ideas and then moved into groups, but many children wanted to work independently since they wanted to express their personal thoughts and feelings. Once the task was outlined clearly, and the necessary structure given, the children were able to suggest a wide range of ideas. It was interesting that Year 3 had to be reminded of what had happened in the first week of their new school.

Implement:
Most children worked independently, but some groups supported each other through the writing. Time was an issue since many children find a written language task difficult. The lower-ability children struggled to produce short letters.

Evaluate and Communicate:
The children enjoyed working as editorial teams and made constructive comments, although they had to be reminded to be tactful! In the whole school, only seven children said that the writing task was their most favourite activity.

Learn from experience:
Children said that they appreciated all the exciting things that were happening in school. They understood the role of an editorial team and how they needed to offer criticism in a helpful way.

How independent were the children? Did they need much support?
This activity highlighted the problems children have with a written activity. As always, a great deal of support and structure was needed by lower-ability children. These children also needed a lot of help to develop their ideas. The higher-ability children obviously coped better with greater independence and skill.

What did staff learn about the children?
Children were far more competent in discussion than in writing, and group leaders were obvious.

What did the children learn about themselves?
Since the children are grouped in sets, they found it easier to contribute and to share ideas. They said that by listening and sharing ideas, they found the task easier.

Any other comments?
This was the only writing activity and the children needed a lot of guidance and help with structure and layout. In the speaking, listening, and drama activities, the children were very confident and they obviously enjoyed these activities far more.

TASC Evaluation

Activity: Mathematics ability

How did the children respond to each segment of the TASC Wheel?

Gather/Organise:
The lower sets needed to revise number bonds to 20. They built a concept map of what they knew. Then they played some traditional number games first (Snap, Ludo, Snakes and Ladders).
The upper sets recalled their understanding of operations well and were able to gather and organise a wealth of information about number games.

Identify, Generate and Decide:
The lower sets worked as a class and drew from their immediate experience of playing the traditional games and generated a number of ideas for their own games. A few ideas were selected and they were eager and excited to think about making one of the games working in small groups.
The upper sets worked from the beginning in groups and identified a wide range of ideas. They then selected the one they thought was the most exciting. The children worked amicably to come to their decision and the ideas were creative and exciting.

Implement:
The lower-ability sets worked with support from classroom assistants and from students and tended to want to make before planning the game.
The upper-ability sets used mathematical language with fluency and understanding, and were able to manipulate across the four rules of number with ease.
Children generally delegated the jobs between the members of the group.

Communicate and Evaluate:
All the children enjoyed making and playing their games. They exchanged games with enthusiasm. They could identify the problems in other games more easily than they could in their own.

Learn from experience:
All the children said how much they had enjoyed creating and playing their game, and allowing other groups to play and evaluate their games. There was extensive discussion of whether the maths in the games was sufficiently challenging. They generally felt that they had worked well in groups and had learned to compromise and adapt their ideas.

How independent were the children? Did they need much support?
The lower-ability sets needed structure and support far more than the upper-ability sets, but all the children were highly motivated and sustained their concentration until they had completed their games.

What did staff learn about the children?
Many of the children needed to be reminded that the maths of the game was more important than the attractive appearance of the game. The lower-ability sets had difficulty in formulating the rules in a written format, so they explained orally. Only a few of the most able children used word problems as the base for their game, but they generally were able to work very logically, and manipulated the four rules of number creatively.

What did the children learn about themselves?
They realised the amount of thinking and planning that goes into designing a game, but were delighted that they could use maths in such a fun way.

Any other comments?
Some children in the upper sets were reluctant to challenge themselves, preferring to play safe. The lower-ability sets produced wonderfully visual games which gave them great delight.

TASC Evaluation

Activity: **Visual/Spatial ability**

How did the children respond to each segment of the TASC Wheel?

Gather/Organise:
Most teachers began with a discussion about the meaning of 'Community', and pupils recognised that the community comprises various groups of people who all have the need for relaxation and fun.

Identify:
Children were eager to suggest ideas for various age groups, and although they were keen to develop a 'fun place' for their own age group, they were also willing to consider older and younger members of the community.

Generate:
Some children obviously need to develop greater concentration in listening to others, but generally the children engaged in lengthy discussion and came up with creative ideas.

Decide:
Most children worked in pairs or small groups, a few worked individually. They prioritised their ideas and decided on the necessary amenities. This brought issues of safety and comfort into the discussion.

Implement:
All children were focused on the task and enjoyed the activity. There were no behaviour problems and children worked cooperatively, evaluating their ideas as they worked. Some groups offered to assist others with advice and practical help. Some children worked in 3D, others drew a plan or a design. Some children managed the extension task of producing an enlargement of one section.

Evaluate and Communicate:
Children were keen to appreciate others' work and to make constructive comments about designs and ideas.

Learn from experience:
The children expressed great enjoyment of this activity and decided that they had worked very well together. Some children said they would include more detail next time and others commented on how they could improve their plans, some said they would plan the use of their time better, or that they would consider a fun place for a mixed community.

How independent were the children? Did they need much support?
The children were self-motivated and generally needed little support. Some children needed help to crystallise their decisions. They were very supportive of each other.

What did staff learn about the children?
Some of the most creative ideas were not always the most visually appealing. Many of the 'less able' children produced very good plans and designs and they enjoyed the activity.

What did the children learn about themselves?
They said how useful it was to share ideas and that all members of a community are important. They also said that they had learned how to plan, how to share out tasks, and how to work together as a team.

Any other comments?
This was a favourite activity across the ability range, and all children were focused on the task. Most children were very pleased with their work and they had used a variety of media very effectively and creatively.

So, at the end of an exciting and fulfilling TASC Week, it was time for reflection – to *learn from experience*.

Reflection on Phase 3

- Staff were left in no doubt that the children preferred to learn in a very practical way. The entire week was full of high motivation, excitement and enjoyment, and members of staff were tired but exhilarated! They discussed how much they had learned about the children's abilities. Although the week's activities had provided only a snapshot of each child, the staff intend to continue to build up a more informed profile of each child through the year.

- We have always realised the importance of building the emotional, social and spiritual strength of each child, but presenting such a wide range of activities highlighted the need to help each child to respond to new activities with confidence; to react in a group situation with ease and understanding of other children's needs; and to work cooperatively with others.

- We realised that each of the multiple abilities cannot function discretely and alone: while an activity may reflect the dominant characteristics of that activity, there is always an interplay with other abilities – particularly the social, emotional and spiritual abilities.

- Upper Key Stage 2 pupils are far more capable of tackling open-ended activities than lower Key Stage 2 pupils who need far more structured support. However, it is important to provide regular opportunities for all children to develop their problem-solving abilities by posing open-ended challenges.

- TASC Week emphasised the talents of all our children. Though we routinely celebrate the successes of all children in subjects across the curriculum, it reminded us not to underestimate the creativity and ingenuity of those children who do not shine in their written work.

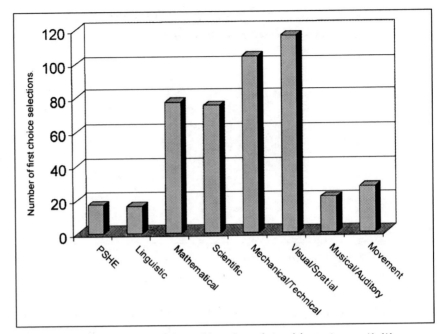

Figure 4.11 Whole-school profile of preferred learning activities

Human Abilities	Tom	Bradley	Dwayne	Dale	Martyn	Harry D	Natasha	Grace	Harley	Jessica G	Charlie	Laura	Eleanor	Rosie	Harry L	Joshua Mt	Joshua Ml	Jessica M	Stephanie	Thomas	George	Alice	Lauren R	Aaron	Adam	Lauren W	Jack
Linguistic	5	6	8	5	4	8	3	6	6	8	5	8	1	8	6	8	6	8	8	4	3	4		4	3	5	3
Mathematical	4	3	2	4	1	2	2	2	2	5	4	2	4	2	3	3	3	6	2	1	2	5		7	1	4	2
Scientific	3	5	3	3	3	3	7	5	8	6	6	4	3	3	2	7	4	2	3	5	5	2		8	5	6	1
Mechanical	2	4	5	2	2	5	4	7	7	4	3	3	5	1	1	4	1	5	5	8	6	3		6	6	7	4
Visual/Spatial	1	1	1	1	7	1	1	1	1	1	1	1	1	2	6	4	1	2	4	1	3	1	1	1	2	1	6
Musical	6	2	6	6	6	6	6	4	3	3	7	5	8	4	5	2	5	3	7	6	4	6		2	7	2	5
Movement	7	7	7	8	8	7	5	3	5	2	2	7	7	5	8	6	7	1	4	2	7	7		5	4	3	7
PSHE	8	8	4	7	5	4	8	8	4	7	8	6	6	7	7	5	8	7	6	7	8	8		3	8	8	8

Figure 4.12 A class profile of preferred learning activities
(1 = most preferred; 8 = least preferred)

Figures 4.11 and 4.12 show the preferred learning activities of the whole school and of a single class respectively. The Visual/Spatial activity proved to be most popular. The children enjoyed designing and making their fun places. They considered their attempts to be successful. The Linguistic activity rated lowest in the children's overall preferences. This was perhaps mainly due to the fact that it was the only *written* activity. Perhaps a linguistic activity centred on speaking and listening would have yielded a different result, although the discussion-based PSHE activity also came very low in the children's ranking. However, in an analysis such as that above, it is important not to make global assumptions based on the children's experience of one activity. There are other factors which would need to be analysed such as: the emotional mood of the children on the particular day; the style, approach and methods of teaching; the physical conditions in the classroom or hall, etc.

Reflective comments by the staff

Conclusion and the way forward

- We will plan to include far more practical, hands-on activities throughout the year, since pupils are so excited, motivated and attentive when they are learning through practical activities.

- We discovered a few children in every class, who had previously been relatively unnoticed, but who came alive during our DISCOVER/TASC Week. They absolutely shone and radiated life through activities that did not depend on writing skills. While continuing to develop their essential writing skills, we will make sure that their inner light keeps ablaze, and that they continue to have opportunities to demonstrate their abilities and experience joy in high achievement within their ability strengths.

- We will continue to focus on the essential skills of Literacy, and although we already teach a wide range of recording skills in this area, we will create more opportunities for *all* children to implement and communicate their ideas across the full range of multiple abilities.

- Our team of Learning Support Assistants attend all our INSET training sessions and are invaluable assets to the school. They use the DISCOVER/TASC Approach as a structure for thinking and doing activities with the children who need special support.

- We now need to consolidate and extend our new skills of teaching and learning. We will continue to organise our DISCOVER/TASC Weeks; and we will continue to thread the TASC Process and the DISCOVER problem types throughout our lesson planning. However, we also realise that members of staff vary in their personal styles, and take on the TASC Approach in varying degrees. Also, we realise that teachers new to the school will need support and help from senior members of staff who will act as mentors.

An Action Research Project at Claremont Primary School

SIMON CHANDLER

Many children have to overcome potentially debilitating factors in their young lives, and many teachers are helping these young learners towards self-respect, self-confidence and mastery of their learning. Teachers do matter to children: they can and do make a difference between failure and success, despair and joy, excitement and disillusion. As adults we all remember the teachers who made us feel worthwhile and valued, who gave us broad horizons, who motivated us to persevere. Yes, teachers really can make a difference and light up learners from within.

(Belle Wallace)

Background

Claremont[1] Primary School's catchment draws mainly from a low socio-economic area in a large housing estate in a small town. In September 1998, the school had been declared from a previous Ofsted inspection to have 'serious weaknesses'. The former management of the school had been criticised and the self-esteem and morale of the staff was low. On taking up appointment as the new head teacher in September 2000, I set myself the task of empowering staff, developing both staff and

---

1 'Claremont' is a pseudonym, and all the photographs and examples of children's work used in this chapter are from 'Claremont' School.

pupil motivation, and renovating the whole school building which was dilapidated, cluttered, drab and discouraging. I knew that we had to work as a team, involving staff, pupils and parents in setting our joint goals, working out plans to reach those goals but, at the same time, setting achievable targets which would not overburden staff.

Whole-school development (Phase 1)

In October 2000, the 'brown envelope' arrived announcing the date of our next Ofsted inspection, and this galvanised us into action. We concentrated on enhancing our pupils' personal development, raising self-esteem, lifting the school culture to embrace a positive celebration of pupil strengths and diversity. By the end of our first year, the Parent–Teacher Association had raised enough money for us to renovate the whole school. Pupils pored over samples of curtain fabrics, made an initial selection and then conducted a survey to find out which fabrics were preferred. The pupils also conducted a survey to decide which were their favourite colours (the result of which is our newly painted blue and yellow hall!). The old 1970s' orangey-brown window blinds were replaced with light textured vertical blinds, again selected by the children. The children's attitude to school changed overnight! The graffiti disappeared from the refurbished areas and the pupils began keeping their classrooms clean and tidy. The teachers also enjoyed a comfortable, well-furnished staffroom for the first time.

We felt passionate about creating a learning environment which celebrated all children's achievements, allowed children to learn using a variety of learning styles, and to view their mistakes as learning points. When we were introduced to the TASC Framework, we welcomed the fact that it provided a coherent umbrella that allowed us to make educational decisions we understood and could incorporate into the National Curriculum Framework. We reorganised our planning teams so that teachers worked together to plan for Foundation, Key Stage 1, Years 3 and 4, and Years 5 and 6. This allowed us to look at continuity, to remove repetition, and to focus on exciting activities.

We decided to introduce TASC to the children initially through half-term history topics: 'The Greeks' with Years 5 and 6; 'The Tudors' with Years 3 and 4; and 'Toys' with Key Stage 1. A teacher from a nearby school where they were already using the TASC Framework spent the morning with us sharing her school's experience and answering our queries, and we spent the afternoon planning.

'The Tudors' (Year 4)

At the end of the projects, the pupils had acquired and were using skills of historical enquiry with ease and confidence. Their intrinsic motivation to learn had improved significantly and parents enquired about how we had 'turned the children on to learning'. Pupils were working in their own time during school and at home, and unauthorised absences dropped dramatically. The children revelled in their ownership of their learning and they organised an exhibition of all their work that was the trigger for a whole-school celebration to which parents were invited.

Comments made by parents and governors at the exhibition

This is a fantastic display! I never thought the children could do this sort of work.

The children are really excited and motivated, and didn't want to stop!

They are really interested in history for the first time.

Comments made by teachers in their reflection on the experience

Comments made by the pupils

I love going to school now...
I like working on a group project because I like
working with other people... Mr Chandler came
to our class and he taught us all how to be relaxed
and calm before we start a lesson or even before a
test like SATs. The classrooms are really nice now –
the next job is the toilets... Thank you for reading
this and I hope that my report helps.

The school has been improved...
it's been painted and coloured up. The
rooms are nice and bright and happy
now... Now we would like some new
playground toys, 4 swings, 2 sets of
monkey bars, 1 or 2 slides, and
some balls and ropes.

Assemblies are better now
because we have a chance to
state our opinions. I think asking
pupils is a good way to make
things better.

The school link inspector carried out interviews with Year 6 pupils and this is a summary of the general points the children made.

What do you like about school?

- Practical activities
- ICT equipment
- Being consulted
- A good physical environment
- Working independently and also with others

What don't you like?

- Repetition
- Non-demanding activities
- Problems with the physical aspects of the school

What would you improve?

- More group work
- More equipment

● Have a homework room

● Have a range of clubs with proper trainers

● More fun and relaxation with our learning

Whole-school development (Phase 2)

The staff decided that they wanted to extend their work using TASC to include activities incorporating the full range of human abilities more systematically. The staff would observe and possibly begin to assess the children's abilities, and the children would discuss their preferred activities at the end of the week. Consequently, several twilight sessions were used for discussion and planning. It was decided to hold a week of activities organised around the human abilities incorporating:

● Visual/Spatial ability

● Mathematical/Symbolic ability

● Mechanical/Technical ability

● Social, Emotional and Spiritual abilities

● Linguistic/Symbolic ability

● Scientific/Realistic ability

● Movement/Somatic ability

● Auditory/Sonal ability

The activities needed to accommodate a whole class at the same time, and teachers would either work across all the activities with their own classes, or would decide to develop tasks across the year group to suit their personal strengths. Any activity requiring special apparatus that needed to be shared would be timetabled in rotation, for example the use of the hall, the use of the mechanical Lego, the use of musical instruments. Teachers would dovetail the other activities around the core timetable.

Teachers worked as four teams: Reception; Years 1 and 2; Years 3 and 4; Years 5 and 6.

In the following account of the menu of activities, teachers explain in their own words how they planned and carried out the activities. Each group of teachers has reflected on what they learned and how they will adjust where necessary when they run another menu of activities.

Reception

> ☐ 1 class of 16 pupils with teacher and classroom learning assistant.
> ☐ Average length of activity: 20 minutes.
> ☐ Teacher: Becky Williams.

These activities were planned for the first week of the September term and were devised especially to accommodate the needs of early learners, for example the need to work in small groups, the need to accommodate their short attention span, their inability to record their comments. I decided to plan for four activities, each lasting approximately 20 minutes, and I decided to give the children an initial snapshot assessment of 1 to 5, with 3 denoting average performance and 5 denoting excellence. For most activities, I decided that I would make an initial observation of how the children responded without intervention. I intend to make a second assessment after the children have been in school for six weeks. Throughout all the activities, I was observing the children's social and emotional responses.

● *Movement and Auditory abilities combined*

Activity: Identify a variety of animals from pictures, and create sounds and movements to represent them.

We looked at photographs of animals and 'gathered and organised' the names of the animals and the sounds they make. Some children were hearing the animal names for the first time. Then we explored the sounds made by a range of instruments, listened to them carefully and 'decided' which sounds matched which animals the best.

I then made a sound with each of the instruments that had been decided on, and the children 'generated' ideas for moving like each animal in turn.

Teacher reflection

I was able to work with small groups since I had half a class in the morning and half a class in the afternoon so it was easier to observe individual children. All the children in the class responded to matching the sounds with the animals, but although most of the children in the class were able to create movements for the animals, some children obviously lacked prior experience and certainly the confidence to explore the idea.

It was better that I had introduced the animal sounds first because I felt that this had created a good atmosphere for most of the children to feel comfortable enough to respond to the movement activity. In this activity, I referred to the stages of the TASC Wheel orally (the stages correspond well with my teaching style in Reception), but I will introduce the actual TASC Wheel later in the year when the children have gained more confidence, since it takes several weeks for the children to settle to the routines necessary for a smoothly running day.

In this school, with the children who have had little or no experience of a good pre-school, it is obvious that they lack a wide range of experiential learning. I need to develop their learning through rich sensory experiences, to prompt their imagination, and to spend a lot of time developing their language and creative play.

● Visual/Spatial ability

Activity: Draw a picture of the classroom.

I gave the children large sheets of A3 paper and a box of crayons and asked them to draw the classroom. I wanted to see how they spontaneously responded to an open-ended question without being directed as to what to do or shown exactly how to do it. Some children immediately said, 'I don't know how to do it'. So we walked around the classroom, giving everything a name and saying where it was and what it is used for.

Teacher reflection

The children enjoyed the more familiar activity of drawing, but there was a great difference in their perceptions of the task. Some children just scribbled with no transfer of what they had just seen and talked about. One child, however, drew the floor, the ceiling, the walls and endeavoured to place the furniture in the right place around the room.

● Mathematical ability

Activity: Observation of play with boxes of various collections of materials.

I decided to set out boxes of materials to see how the children would respond to them. I set out boxes of animals, small toys, differently coloured rubber dishes, fruit and vegetables, and assorted coloured transparent shapes. Some children were unable to sort even with prompting questions, and they had no beginning concept of counting. Other children spent a long time thinking and then decided to sort the items mostly into colours, with a few children sorting into categories and beginning to count.

Teacher reflection

It was very evident that some children had no experience of sorting and counting, while others were familiar with this kind of situation. The range of pre-school experience is enormously diverse, from very little mathematical experience in its widest sense to obvious sorting and grouping experience. It will be interesting to monitor the development of individual children as their experience widens.

● *Mechanical/Technical ability*

Activity: Observation of play with collections of building materials.

I gave the children sets of Mobilo which contains wheels, axles, and flat, cuboid, rectangular and triangular shapes that can be connected together. The shapes are colourful and easy for young children to handle. I asked them to make something that moved and allowed them to experiment while I observed.

Teacher reflection

It was fascinating to observe the different responses of the children. Again, their abilities varied: some children were able to confidently and independently manipulate the pieces to make something quite complex and moving, while others showed a reluctance to try to assemble the parts even with prompting. Once again the importance of pre-school experience was evident. For some children, it was the first time they had played and manipulated this kind of material.

Years 1–2 and 3–4

Years 1–2

☐ Two classes totalling 58 children.
☐ Teachers: Gill Steeples and Sarah Mitchell.

Years 3–4

☐ Two classes totalling 54 children.
☐ Teachers: Jayne Allen and Ann Sanger.

● *Social, Emotional, Spiritual, and Linguistic abilities*

Activity (Years 1–2): Discussion – What rules do we need to keep everyone safe in school? Design a poster with our most important rule.

We gathered the children's ideas, paraphrasing to develop their language, and feeding in thinking words such as 'generate'. To begin with we had many negative rules such as 'Do not swear', 'Do not kick and bite' and so on, and we tried to encourage the children to think of positive rules:

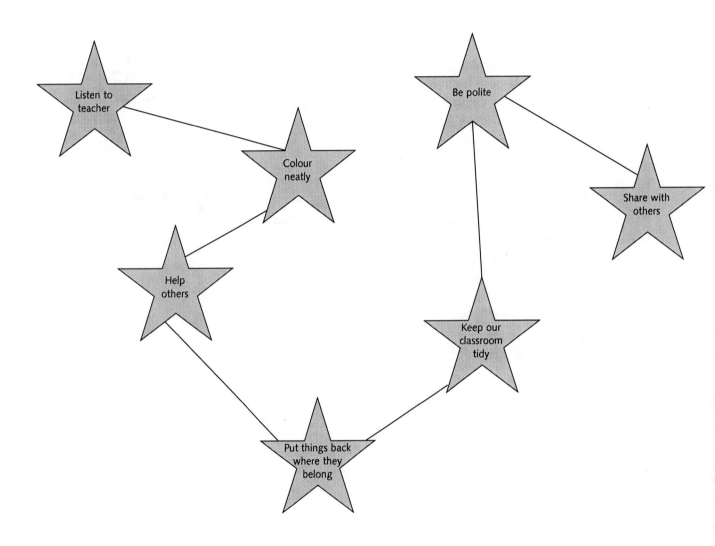

We prioritised the rules using a tick chart and the children then made posters for the classroom.

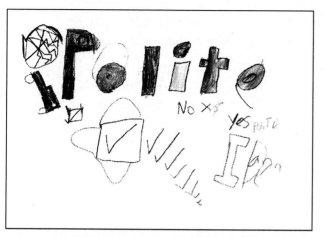

Activity (Years 3–4): What are the most sensible class rules we need? How can we communicate our class rules effectively? This theme of 'understanding and caring' was developed over a half term.

After we discussed and decided on our class rules, we presented an assembly to communicate these to the rest of the school, and the children worked in groups to decide how they would present their ideas. The activities were wide ranging and involved making up a rap, a PowerPoint presentation, a play, a song, posters and a story. We then read a story with the theme of conflict and generated ideas as to how we would solve the conflict. We also continued the theme into a study of Hindu and Sikh cultures, asking the children to identify differences and to generate ideas for harmonious living across cultures.

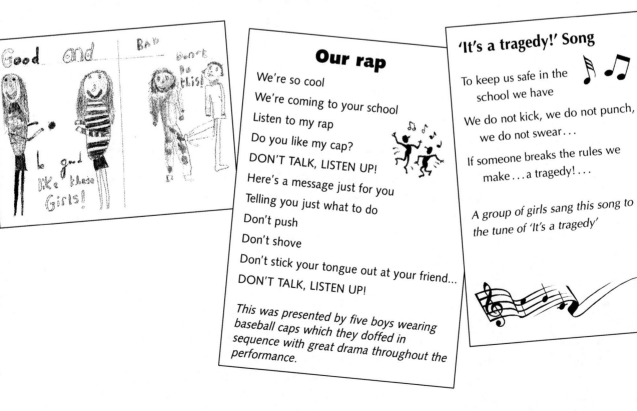

Our rap

We're so cool
We're coming to your school
Listen to my rap
Do you like my cap?
DON'T TALK, LISTEN UP!
Here's a message just for you
Telling you just what to do
Don't push
Don't shove
Don't stick your tongue out at your friend...
DON'T TALK, LISTEN UP!

This was presented by five boys wearing baseball caps which they doffed in sequence with great drama throughout the performance.

'It's a tragedy!' Song

To keep us safe in the school we have

We do not kick, we do not punch, we do not swear...

If someone breaks the rules we make...a tragedy!...

A group of girls sang this song to the tune of 'It's a tragedy'

Teacher reflection

Years 1–2: We realised again the need to concentrate on developing and extending children's language, and the need to focus on the development of oracy as the foundation for reading and writing.

Years 3–4: The major focus of our activity was discussion and sharing ideas, and the children really enjoyed choosing how they would communicate their ideas to the rest of the school. We discovered children who had amazing talent in performing a rap and a song – children who would not shine in Literacy and Numeracy but who excelled in communicating with others.

● *Linguistic ability*

Activity (Years 1–2): Draw a cartoon character with a speech bubble containing a welcome message to the school.

Years 1 and 2 needed a lot of structured support during this activity and it was felt best to limit the task to the cartoon and speech bubble.

Activity (Years 3–4): Design a page for the school magazine.

Years 3 and 4 were able to contribute to the planning of this activity using the TASC Wheel as a guide (see Mindmap 16).

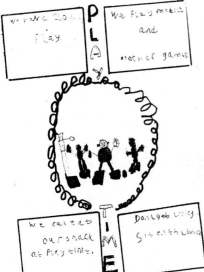

Mindmap 16: Our 'Welcome to school' booklet

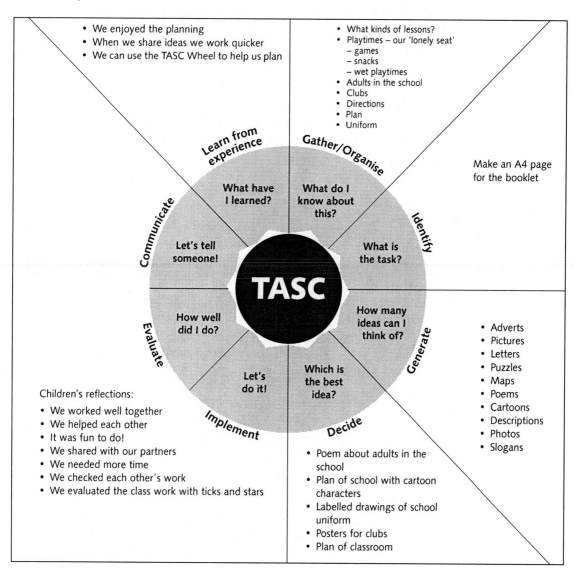

- We enjoyed the planning
- When we share ideas we work quicker
- We can use the TASC Wheel to help us plan

- What kinds of lessons?
- Playtimes – our 'lonely seat'
  – games
  – snacks
  – wet playtimes
- Adults in the school
- Clubs
- Directions
- Plan
- Uniform

Make an A4 page
for the booklet

- Adverts
- Pictures
- Letters
- Puzzles
- Maps
- Poems
- Cartoons
- Descriptions
- Photos
- Slogans

Children's reflections:
- We worked well together
- We helped each other
- It was fun to do!
- We shared with our partners
- We needed more time
- We checked each other's work
- We evaluated the class work with ticks and stars

- Poem about adults in the school
- Plan of school with cartoon characters
- Labelled drawings of school uniform
- Posters for clubs
- Plan of classroom

Teacher reflection

The development of Literacy is a primary target in our school, so we are going to focus on Oracy as the foundation for reading and writing. However, we are very concerned to develop the fullest range of activities so that all children can demonstrate potential across the full range of abilities.

◗ REFLECT

● *Mathematical ability*

Activity (Years 1–2 and 3–4): Make a game to teach counting.

We played a number of mathematical games so that the children would have experience of playing different sorts, and we discussed the rules of each one. Games included: matching and counting cards with shapes; dominoes; snakes and ladders; and a variety of dice

games with shapes, numbers and spots on the faces. After discussing the types of games and the rules for playing each one, the children decided which kind of game they wanted to make and they worked in appropriate groups. We provided support material such as blank number squares and templates for cards and shapes. The children shared their games and explained to each other how their game was played. Although this took the stress off *writing* the rules, the children soon realised how carefully they needed to explain their game. Years 3 and 4 were offered the chance to create more complex games using the four rules of number.

Teacher reflection

The children really enjoyed the sharing of their games and were keen to teach each other how to play them. Two boys produced outstanding games with extended knowledge of number bonds, and also a very good understanding of the purpose of rules. Some children were far less confident and copied others, which again made us realise the importance of developing self-confidence together with the need for rich mathematical, practical experience in which there is an emphasis on fun.

The richness, or otherwise, of children's early learning experiences is certainly reflected in their responses to learning activities provided in the infants' school. Years 3 and 4 were particularly enthusiastic in this activity. Many children came to school early to finish making their game, and we created a games box to store them in. Children were eager to play their games in 'Choosing Time' and 'Golden Time'. When the games were shared, the designers of each game explained the rules to the other players; we avoided the writing down of the rules.

● *Scientific ability*

Activity (Years 1–2 and 3–4): Make a boat to carry as many teddy bears (weights) as possible.

We used simple materials for this activity: one sheet of A4 paper, staples and masking tape.

Teacher reflection

We were surprised at how little the children knew about boats, and had taken it for granted that they would have this background knowledge. If we do this activity again, we will plan a visit to a harbour and gather a collection of model boats and pictures. Nevertheless, after making and testing simple boats, the children were able to suggest improvements to their shapes and designs.

● *Mechanical/Technical ability*

Activity (Years 1–2 and 3–4): Make a vehicle that moves.

We used commercial construction materials like Technical Lego with wheels, levers and gears. We also used cardboard boxes, corrugated paper, wooden wheels, wooden rods, card, art straws, scissors, glue, masking tape and paint.

Teacher reflection

The children had a much greater knowledge base about machines and they made exciting sketches. However, most of their thinking took place when they were turning the sketch of their machines into a working model. Obviously their ideas flowed better when they were using their hands.

We had some surprises! Some of the children who shone as exceptional do not shine in Literacy and Numeracy. All the children responded well to this activity and they all expressed feelings of success; however, not many children could explain *how* their machine moved. Interestingly, the more able children in this activity had constructed from the boxes, card, etc. rather than the commercially produced materials.

● *Visual/Spatial ability*

Activity (Years 1–2 and 3–4): Make a plan of the ideal school.

We explored simple plans and discussed what a plan is. Years 1 and 2 found the concept of a plan very difficult and they drew 2D pictures.

Years 1–2

Even Years 3 and 4 found the *spatial* aspect of this activity difficult, with the exception of one boy who produced a plan that was quite extraordinary.

Years 3–4

● *Auditory/Movement ability*

Activity (Years 1–2 and 3–4): Identify the animals portrayed by the music, and make up movements to represent the animals.

We used excerpts from 'The Carnival of the Animals' (Saint-Saëns). We listened to the music and discussed the kinds of animals the music conveyed. Then the children worked in pairs or alone to produce suitable animal movements.

REFLECT

Teacher reflection

The younger children really enjoyed this activity and worked with energy and enthusiasm. However, there was not much variety of movement and most of the children chose to be lions and elephants. The older children listened intently to the music, and had lots of ideas about the kinds of animals the music suggested, but they were very inhibited about moving like an animal. It needed a lot of encouragement to build their confidence, but they expressed great enjoyment at the end of the lesson.

Years 5 and 6

□ Three classes of mixed Years 5 and 6 (totalling 81 children).

□ Teachers: Maxine Purvis, Ruth Devine and Becky Bason.

In Years 5 and 6, the staff decided to work within their own strengths across the combined year groups, and three teachers shared the ten activities between them. The activities followed the same pattern as for Years 1–2 and 3–4, but obviously the children's responses were more complex.

To avoid undue repetition, we will discuss in detail only the activities based on Auditory/Movement and Mechanical/Technical abilities, since there are some key points in our reflections on these activities.

● *Auditory and Movement abilities combined*

The following two activities were conducted in two successive 30-minute lessons.

Activity 1: Create animal movements using selections from 'The Carnival of the Animals' (Saint-Saëns). Work with your partner(s) to put the movements into a sequence.

Materials: Several contrasting 20-second excerpts from 'The Carnival of the Animals' (a mixture of heavy, deep and light, ethereal music).

Activity 2: Create your own sequence of sounds to represent the animals.

Materials: The full collection of musical instruments with several keyboards and an extensive selection of percussion instruments.

As a new member of staff with a specialism in Physical Education, I (Ruth Devine) realised that the upper classes have generally had very little experience in music and movement due to staffing difficulties in the past. I feared that the older children, especially the boys, would be self-conscious. Many of the pupils have short attention spans and are more than ready to exploit a 'free' situation, so I prepared the activity well before we attempted to create our movements in the hall. It is important to explain the preparation in detail because the response of the children was quite astonishingly on task and very creative, in what is, for them, an unusual activity.

To begin with, each class lay on the floor in a comfortable position while we listened to the music. I asked the children to imagine what kinds of animals the music conveyed to them. Intuitively some children began to respond to the music with feet tapping and heads nodding, while others just lay quietly without moving. Then we 'gathered and organised' what animals the music suggested for the heavy, sombre sequences and the lighter, gentler sequences. We listened to the sequences of music again and I reminded the children that they were listening in order to 'generate' movements by 'imagining them in their heads'. I asked them to 'think about the different styles of moving'. We spent a lot of time listening, talking and exploring ideas and now the children were excited and ready to 'decide on their best movement', practise and perform them.

The pupils chose their own groups of 3 or 4 and then they shared and combined their movements without the music. I timed the group work very tightly: the children chose one sequence from each section of the music (heavy and light) and I allowed only five minutes to work out each sequence; we practised to the music and then demonstrated to each other using the music. I followed on with an additional five minutes for each group to work out the combination of the two sequences – first without and then with the music – and once more we demonstrated to each other.

I followed the Movement activity with the Auditory activity because I felt that the children had the music in their heads and that, since they had responded so well to the Movement activity, they would also respond well to creating the sounds of the animals. First we 'gathered and organised' the sounds of the instruments into categories corresponding to the animals they had portrayed in the Movement activity. Each group chose one instrument to make the sound of their animal then we gradually added other instruments one by one, discussing the power of a single sound in relation to a sequence or combination of sounds, and harmony in relation to discord.

REFLECT (**Children's reflections**

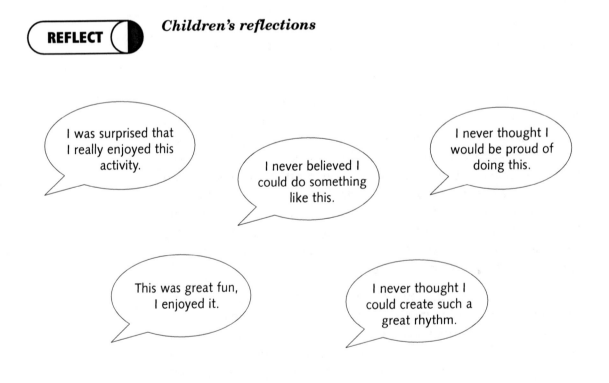

Teacher reflection

In the Movement activity, some of the children were extremely fluent and creative in their movements, while others were restricted and stilted. But I was surprised that every pupil responded so well, even if it was only with heavy plodding, repetitive elephant movements. There were no 'behavioural' incidents because every pupil was focusing on the task, but I'm sure that this was because we had done so much listening and talking at the start of the session and the children were well prepared to implement the task. I intend to start a movement/gymnastics/music club since the children responded so enthusiastically.

I was also surprised at the quality and variety of sound rhythms the children produced. When I introduced body sounds, they responded well to those too. I used the same idea when we were studying Asian culture; we listened to Asian music, discussed the sounds and rhythms, and then created our own Asian music. The children responded enthusiastically and said how much they enjoyed the lesson.

Since the older pupils do very little movement and music, I think it was a good idea to structure the lesson tightly, while still allowing pupils to explore, choose, make decisions and share their finished effort. It was equally important to give the children a chance to reflect on the activity, and the consequent sharing of their enjoyment of the lesson led to a positive whole peer-group attitude and acceptance that working with Movement and Sounds is an enjoyable activity.

● *Mechanical/Technical ability*

Activity: Make something that moves.

Materials: Commercial mechanical construction materials, cardboard, tin cans, plastic bottles, wooden dowels, wheels, art straws, elastic bands, string, balloons, Sellotape™, glue, split pins.

There was potential here for chaos! With so many materials lying around the classroom and pupils inclined to become over-excited very easily, again I (Ruth Devine) decided to structure the lesson carefully, while still allowing pupils enough freedom to think for themselves. Since the children do very little creative making from junk materials, I began by asking the children to 'gather and organise' the possible pitfalls they might encounter with regard to using and joining different materials. We discussed a variety of techniques for paper and card engineering such as ways of making strong joints, suitable glues and fixing materials, how to make slits and reinforce edges, etc. We did this quite quickly, with myself or a child demonstrating the techniques.

We 'generated' ideas for our things that could move, stressing that 'big and grand' doesn't necessarily mean 'the best'. The pupils sketched out their plans, decided on the best idea and began to make their constructions. I observed that many of the children were very ingenious and learned inventively as their structures took shape.

Case study 1

Wendy is a very shy and solitary child, apparently very self-contained and seemingly content to be in the background. As the week's menu of activities progressed, she was smiling more often, volunteering ideas and offering to do jobs. As the term has progressed, since I have been integrating the TASC way of working, she has shown greater independence, her work has generally improved and she is altogether brighter and more responsive.

Case study 2

Sally has always been painfully silent and withdrawn. As the week progressed, she began to express her thoughts and ideas, and although still very shy, she put up her hand to volunteer an idea — something she has never done before. I'm sure it was partly due to the message of the whole week that everyone has ideas that are worthwhile and acceptable, and that no-one is wrong.

Case study 3

Damien can seldom focus on a task and his work in Literacy and Numeracy is well below standard, very untidy and seldom completed. He often needs 'one-to-one restraint' and is generally disruptive in class. He was focused on task for the entire morning, even through the playtime, and worked alone to produce the most amazing and complex machine. He was obviously very proud to be told that his machine was fantastic! His machine took pride of place in the school exhibition.

Children's reflections

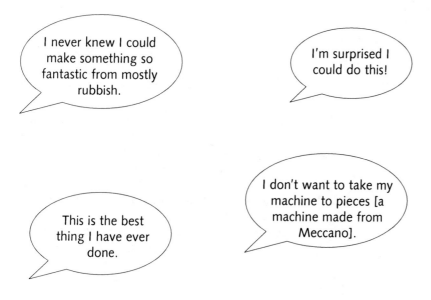

I never knew I could make something so fantastic from mostly rubbish.

I'm surprised I could do this!

This is the best thing I have ever done.

I don't want to take my machine to pieces [a machine made from Meccano].

Teacher reflection

We realised that the children need regular experiences of this kind of creative inventing and making. They tended to become very noisy and excited, and we realised that the children have little chance to do this kind of practical creative designing and making either at home or at school. The children talked about this experience for a long time afterwards and it was obviously one of the highlights of the week. The TASC Wheel helped both the children and the teachers to focus sharply on the processes of thinking about and creating a machine.

Conclusion: Overall reflection of teachers with regard to the week's activities

Over the week, we could assess the children's skills of 'learning how to learn'. We could see how well they approached, coped with and completed a range of open-ended tasks, and how much support and structure they needed to carry out the task. Many children, especially the older ones, confidently used the TASC Wheel to support their thinking processes. Others needed to be reminded, but then referred to the particular stage of the TASC Wheel to support their thinking process.

We could assess the strengths and weaknesses of their general social and emotional skills and their skills of interaction when working with others. It was clear which children could work cooperatively and which children needed more guidance and control. Also it became evident that some children preferred to work alone, or had to work alone because they were not chosen as a partner or included in a group. We were able to see which children were self-confident and which children were tentative and anxious when asked to think for themselves.

The initial activities provided a snapshot of each pupil that can be developed and expanded throughout the term.

Pupils were highly motivated to complete the tasks and expressed great enjoyment of the whole week. Many expressed thoughts which conveyed that they had greater understanding of their thinking and way of working: 'I now know that I need someone to help me gather my ideas. But it's better that I work on my own for the *doing* part of the activity.'

For many children, especially the younger ones, we need to be explicit in the wording of the tasks. The lower-ability children need structured support and often struggle with a task unless the stages are carefully outlined; but they still related to the stages of the TASC Wheel. More able and older children soon learn to work independently using the TASC Wheel to guide their thinking.

In our school, with the younger children, the TASC Wheel needs to be presented using simple words to begin with, gradually building in the more complex thinking words as the children gain understanding and confidence.

We need to give the children time to settle into their new classes at the beginning of the new year. They need the classroom routine to be established, so organising the activities would be better after about six weeks of settling in.

The children loved the practical tasks and enjoyed learning through the hands-on experiences.

Some of the activities such as the Mechanical/Technical ones and those activities expressed through the performing arts, revealed unexpected hidden depths of many children. Often these children were not among the more able in Literacy and Numeracy.

The children tend to get excited over so much 'free practical work', and we needed more parents to help us. But the parents would need to be asked not to do the task *for* the children, but just to lend the 'use of their hands' for difficult tasks. The children would still need to do the thinking.

We will continue to use the TASC Approach for our topic work which we spread over half a term, and we will be more aware of the need to provide opportunities for the children to express ideas across the full range of multiple abilities. At the same time, we will be aware of opportunities to use the TASC Approach in aspects of all lessons, while maintaining the need for lessons that introduce new skills, practise skills and tackle specific areas of the National Curriculum.

Appendix 1

Appendix 1A

Practical teacher observation checklist outlining
general problem solving abilities (identified through
DISCOVER/TASC observations)

- Ideas are used by other children
- Recalls strategies
- Transfers strategies
- Sees connections
- Reflects on own performance
- Suggests improvements
- Explains and justifies
- Discusses similarities and differences
- Monitors own progress

- Makes several groupings of ideas and things
- Invents strategies for problem-solving
- Develops others' ideas
  - Understands task quickly
    - Distinguishes important features
      - Organises materials
      - Generates several ideas
        - Needs minimum explanation
        - Explains task easily

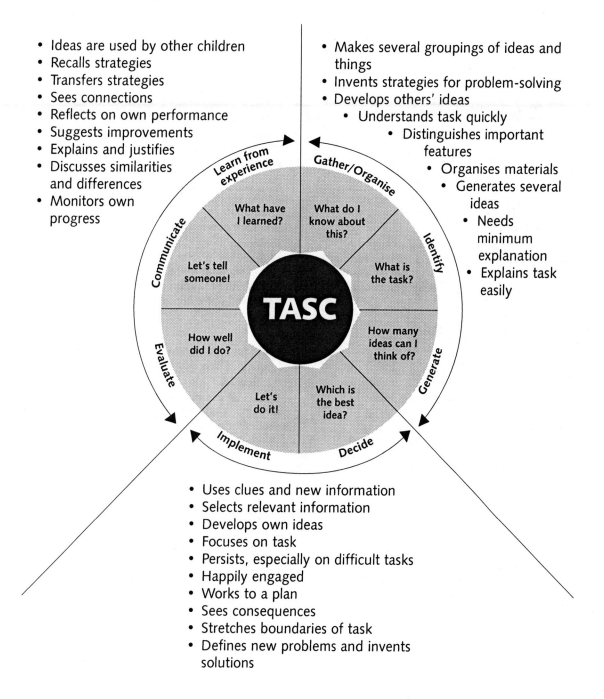

- Uses clues and new information
- Selects relevant information
- Develops own ideas
- Focuses on task
- Persists, especially on difficult tasks
- Happily engaged
- Works to a plan
- Sees consequences
- Stretches boundaries of task
- Defines new problems and invents solutions

© Belle Wallace and June Maker (2004) *Thinking Skills and Problem-Solving – An Inclusive Approach*, David Fulton Publishers, with acknowledgement to Karen Collins and Usanee Anuruthwong.

Appendix 1A.i

Practical teacher observational checklist outlining the core characteristics specific to each human ability

EARLY YEARS SPECIFIC PROBLEM-SOLVING ABILITIES

NOTE: These characteristics are in line with the Foundation Stage Profile and Key Stage 1 (UK).

1. Social Potential **Characteristics:** • shows empathy with others • gets on well with others • shows patience with others • involves or considers others in decision-making • considers others when expressing own feelings • leads and/or follows as appropriate	**Activities for observation:** • games involving other people • cooperative play activities • playground behaviour • dance, drama and mime activities • small group work
2. Emotional Potential **Characteristics:** • identifies and describes own feelings • identifies causes and effects of own feelings • expresses and releases negative emotions • sees the effects of expressing emotions in certain ways	**Activities for observation:** • discussions about behaviour of characters in stories • games • dance, drama and mime activities • playground behaviour • discussions about highly emotional topics
3. Spiritual Potential **Characteristics:** • aware of reactions of others (also social) • concerned about 'fair play' • settles arguments (also social) • is a peacemaker • asks questions about living and dying • shows openness to all points of view on religious questions • wonders about universal questions	**Activities for observation:** • cooperative activities • discussions of social behaviour • drama and role-play activities • playing or working in groups • discussions of moral dilemmas
4. Linguistic Potential **Characteristics:** • uses advanced vocabulary with understanding • can use prepositions and comparisons to explain connections between ideas • shows understanding in dual language • often has a dialogue with the print • discusses a story at length	**Activities for observation:** • telling a story from pictures • playing word and picture games • telling a story with fluency and expression • performing detailed 'show and tell' • recalling an event with detail

5. Mathematical Potential

Characteristics:

- retains what is learned and can apply learning to solve mathematical problems
- solves complex mathematical puzzles
- creates unusual patterns
- sees relationships and connections among numbers, symbols and/or shapes
- remembers sequences of numbers and symbols
- can work forwards and backwards through a sequence
- makes mathematical comparisons

Activities for observation:

- pattern and shape puzzles
- matching and sorting puzzles
- weighing and measuring problems
- games of logic
- games of strategy

6. Scientific Potential

Characteristics:

- likes experimenting with plants, animals, chemicals, or environments
- notices fine details in natural phenomena
- likes solving science problems
- builds and makes models of scientific information or ideas
- spots inconsistencies

Activities for observation:

- collecting and grouping things
- investigation activities
- sequence activities
- building and making models

7. Mechanical/Technical Potential

Characteristics:

- takes things apart
- enjoys building and making devices
- wants to see the inside workings of things
- fixes machines or devices

Activities for observation:

- Lego and Multifix activities
- designing and drawing activities
- using toys with moving parts
- building and making activities

8. Visual/Spatial Potential

Characteristics:

- solves hands-on problems easily
- spots visual similarities and differences
- creates unusual visual patterns
- constructs or draws with detail and perspective
- spends a long time looking at pictures, diagrams, maps

Activities for observation:

- do and make activities
- building activities
- drawing and painting activities
- 3D, tangram and jigsaw puzzles

9. Auditory Potential

Characteristics:

- responds to melody and rhythm
- distinguishes sounds and tones accurately
- learns melodies easily
- shows observable responses to different musical modes
- recognises when voices or instruments are 'in tune'

Activities for observation:

- dance and drama activities
- song and band activities
- clapping and rhythm games
- musical games
- listening activities

10. Somatic/Physical Potential

Characteristics:

- has good hand–eye coordination
- moves with grace and fluency
- moves creatively
- controls gross- and fine-motor movement
- has accurate sense of timing and direction
- changes pace smoothly
- distinguishes flavours accurately
- distinguishes tastes accurately without looking
- mimes with accuracy and expression

Activities for observation:

- games requiring large- or fine-motor movement
- obstacle courses
- dance, drama and mime activities
- hand–eye coordination activities
- tactile boxes
- taste samples

Appendix 1A.ii

Practical teacher observational checklist outlining the core characteristics specific to each human ability

KEY STAGE 2 SPECIFIC PROBLEM-SOLVING ABILITIES

NOTE: These characteristics are in line with the Key Stage 2 (UK) National Curriculum Framework.

1. Social Potential	
Characteristics: • shows empathy with others • understands rules and guidelines • sees cause and effect of happenings • involves or considers others in decision-making • considers others when expressing own feelings • leads and/or follows as appropriate	**Activities for observation:** • games involving other people • role-play activities • playground behaviour • dance, drama and mime activities • small group work • discussions of issues and behaviour
2. Emotional Potential	
Characteristics: • identifies and describes own feelings • identifies causes and effects of own feelings • expresses and releases negative emotions • sees the effects of expressing emotions in certain ways	**Activities for observation:** • discussions about behaviour of characters in stories • games • dance, drama and mime activities • playground behaviour • discussions about highly emotional topics
3. Spiritual Potential	
Characteristics: • understands symbolism • concerned about 'fair play' • settles arguments (also social) • is a peacemaker • asks questions about human values • shows openness to all points of view on religious questions • wonders about universal questions	**Activities for observation:** • cooperative activities • discussions of social behaviour • drama and role-play activities • playing or working in groups • discussions of moral dilemmas
4. Linguistic Potential	
Characteristics: • uses advanced vocabulary and structures accurately and creatively • can use complex structures to sequence and explain ideas • shows understanding in dual language • empathises with characters and issues • identifies differences in purposes and styles	**Activities for observation:** • summarising a story extracting key points • devising word games • telling a story with fluency and expression • performing drama and role play • recalling an event with detail

5. Mathematical Potential

Characteristics:

- remembers and generalises mathematical rules
- solves multiple-step problems
- uses unusual sequences
- sees relationships and connections among numbers, symbols and/or shapes
- investigates patterns or sequences
- can work forwards and backwards through a sequence
- makes mathematical comparisons

Activities for observation:

- multi-level pattern and shape puzzles
- multiple criteria matching and sorting puzzles
- open-ended, multiple-step problems
- games of logic
- games of strategy

6. Scientific Potential

Characteristics:

- likes experimenting with plants, animals, chemicals, or environments
- notices fine details in natural phenomena
- see connections, collects data, uses evidence
- builds and makes models of scientific information or ideas
- spots inconsistencies

Activities for observation:

- collecting and grouping things
- investigation activities
- sequence activities
- building and making models

7. Mechanical/Technical Potential

Characteristics:

- uses tools and techniques with accuracy
- manipulates techniques creatively
- enjoys building and making devices
- manipulates shapes, rotation, angles
- fixes machines or devices

Activities for observation:

- Lego and Multifix activities
- designing, making and drawing activities
- making and manipulating moving structures

8. Visual/Spatial Potential

Characteristics:

- solves hands-on problems easily
- spots visual similarities and differences
- experiments with techniques and methods
- constructs or draws with unusual detail and perspective
- uses shapes, textures, tones creatively
- experiments with 2D and 3D ideas

Activities for observation:

- construction/design activities
- observation activities
- drawing, painting, texture and tactile activities
- multi-level 3D, tangram and jigsaw puzzles

9. Auditory Potential

Characteristics:

- responds to melody, rhythm and beat
- interprets sounds and tones accurately
- learns melodies easily
- recognises moods and qualities of sounds
- recognises voices and body music as expressive instruments

Activities for observation:

- dance and drama activities
- song and band activities
- clapping and rhythm games
- musical games
- listening activities

10. Somatic/Physical Potential

Characteristics:

- has accurate sense of space, speed, direction and shape
- links movements and sequences fluently
- has wide repertoire of skills and movements
- has good control of gross and fine movement
- responds to flavours and textures accurately
- mimes with accuracy and expression
- expresses feeling, moods, ideas expressively

Activities for observation:

- games requiring large- or fine-motor movement
- obstacle courses
- dance, drama and mime activities
- multi-sequence movements
- taste and texture puzzles

© Belle Wallace and June Maker (2004) *Thinking Skills and Problem-Solving – An Inclusive Approach*, David Fulton Publishers, with acknowledgement to Karen Collins and Usanee Anuruthwong.

Appendix 1B

Introducing a TASC Problem-solving Day

First steps

Before planning a menu of activities across the full range of the ten human abilities, it is a good idea to introduce the TASC Wheel through a TASC Problem-solving Day. A number of schools have developed the following ideas:

- Design and make a 'Thinking Skills' hat.

- Create something unusual from a 2-litre plastic bottle.

- Create something unusual from one, or a collection, of cereal cartons.

- Make a Guy Fawkes, a scarecrow, or an 'alien'.

The children gather together newspapers and magazines, 2-litre plastic bottles, cereal cartons, scraps of card, and the school supplies scissors, masking tape, glue, coloured paper, paint, scraps of fabric and all kinds of things that can be used for making. The children work to the stages of the TASC Wheel to make their artefacts, either working in pairs, small groups or independently. The day concludes with a celebration of everyone's artefact displayed in the school hall for parents, and the children explain to their parents the purpose of the day. Inevitably, there is great excitement!

When the children have experienced working to the Problem-solving Framework of the TASC Wheel, they can then be guided to apply and use the Wheel in their activities across the ten human abilities.

Planning a menu of activities across the multiple abilities

In this part of the appendix we provide suggestions for practical activities that allow children to display the essential characteristics within each human ability.

Firstly, here are some notes with regard to developing and implementing the practical activities across the full range of human abilities:

● The following activities took place during a week of term. The normal timetable was suspended and the children worked through the activities throughout the week. Some activities took place in rotation in the school hall, while others took place in the normal classroom.

● In a busy classroom of 30 pupils, the introductory activities can only provide *snapshots* of pupils' affinities and abilities. The snapshots need to be extended and refined through further similar activities throughout the year. Teachers have said that through the initial activities, they have gained a *general overview* of children's abilities across the full range of activities. They have been able to observe children who are outstanding within an ability and children who have great difficulty within an ability. However, we need to emphasise again the *snapshot* quality of this initial observation. Also, after each activity it is essential to sit with the children in 'circle' time and reflect on their feelings and thoughts about the activity.

● The Framework of the TASC Problem-solving Wheel is used to carry out each activity and most of the thinking and discussing is oral. Sometimes each stage of the Problem-solving Process is quite short, and sometimes the children think and practise through doing, trialling and improving.

● Classroom assistants are important observers and facilitators. Parents can also be important observers but they need to be encouraged to refrain from *doing* the activities *for* the younger children in the mistaken belief that they are helping. Children only need help when they are frustrated by their lack of competence with the practical tasks such as cutting or sticking. Then a helper can say, 'You do all the thinking and tell me exactly what to do. How would you like my pair of big hands to help you?' Then the helper needs to give only the help that is necessary before letting the child carry on independently. Children with special learning needs, however, should be given as much structure and help as they need to move them into action and doing.

- General problem-solving abilities can be observed during all the practical activities as well as particular abilities across the full range of human abilities. However, many of the practical activities combine characteristics across several human abilities. It is not possible to work only within one ability: for example, skill in completing mathematical puzzles or word games is accompanied by huge emotional enjoyment and fun; while building or making something may call upon Mechanical/ Technical ability but also involves Visual/Spatial, Movement, Mathematical and Scientific abilities.

- It is advisable to settle a new class and to develop classroom routines of acceptable behaviour and expectations since the children tend to become excited when they experience a range of activities that are often quite different from their usual school activities.

- In the trials of the following activities in schools, teachers have refined the original menu of suggestions to suit their children and to accommodate their own strengths or otherwise. In one school, for example, every teacher engaged in the whole range of activities with her or his class; in another school, specialist teachers engaged in certain activities such as music and movement with the whole year group. However, all teachers were involved in the pre-planning and post-discussions. The following activities are only broad suggestions. All the activities need to be adjusted to suit the cultural and learning backgrounds of the pupils.

- Schools have organised the menu of activities throughout one week so that certain materials such as Technical Lego could be shared and the use of the school hall could be timetabled. Activities were timetabled for different amounts of time, for example the practical making activities needed more time than the movement activity.

Examples of activities

The activities are only outlined here, and Chapters 4 and 5 describe how the range of activities have been developed and implemented in two schools. For all of the activities, pupils can work as a class or in small groups.

Social, Emotional, Spiritual

NOTE: Social, emotional and spiritual ability can be observed throughout all other activities. But the three abilities can be grouped together for an initial 'snapshot' using one of the following activities.

Activities:

- Discuss rules for acceptable behaviour in school. Design a poster to advertise one rule.

- Discuss rules of fair play in the playground. Decide how you can monitor playground behaviour.

- Take a school issue (e.g. running the tuck shop, organising a parents' evening, setting up an exhibition) and allow the children to make decisions and carry them through to action.

Linguistic

Activity: Write a poem or a letter to someone who might be new in your school to tell them what you like best about your school OR Tell your friend about the best day you have had in school.

The second activity is oral and can be used with young children who are not yet writing, or with children who have difficulties with writing things down. In these cases, a scribe who is an older Year 5/6 child, or a parent can help.

Mathematical

Activity: Make a game to teach someone how to add up to 10 or 20.

Basic materials: Card, coloured paper, rulers, crayons and/or paint, masking tape, glue, scissors.

This maths game can be for individuals, pairs or small groups, and it can be adjusted to suit the age and ability of classes from Years 1 to 6. For example, older, more able children can make a game to teach the four rules of number, while other children will need more help to structure a simpler game and will also need assistance if they are asked to write down the rules of the game.

Scientific

Activity: Design and make a boat which will carry the most weight.

Basic materials: A4 sheets of newspaper, masking tape, scissors, glue, 10 g weights, bowl(s) or sink to test the boats.

Children need to design and make their first boat, test it, and then have the chance to redesign, make and test again.

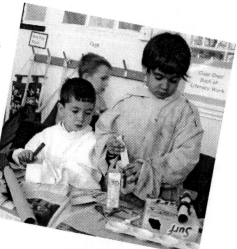

Mechanical/Technical

Activity: Make a machine that moves.

Basic materials: Technical Lego, Unifix Cubes with wheels, or other mechanical/technical kits. If this is not possible, a collection of card, glue, scissors, masking tape, art straws and small wheels will do.

The only criterion is that the machine must move in some way, but how it moves depends on the ingenuity and creativity of the children.

Visual/Spatial

Activity: Design and make a place for people to have fun.

Basic materials: Card, coloured paper, rulers, crayons and/or paint, masking tape, glue, scissors.

Children can decide whether they make a fun place for families or just for children. 2D or 3D fun places are acceptable although the children need to decide this for themselves.

Auditory

Activity: Use conventional and unusual instruments to create animal sounds.

Basic materials: As many different sound-making instruments as is possible.

The children can listen to, or make up their own simple story about animals engaged in typical daily routines. Then ask the children to introduce some conflict, for example: a cat chasing a bird, a fox getting into the hens' yard, elephants stampeding.

Somatic/Physical

Activity: Make up walks for toys or animals to suit the music OR Make up training exercises for sports to suit the music.

Basic materials: Two or more pieces of contrasting music each lasting 20 seconds, for example: sections from 'Peter and the Wolf' (Prokofiev), 'The Carnival of the Animals' (Saint-Saëns).

Use culturally appropriate music but try to ensure that the music has opportunities for contrasting movements. Children work in small groups and demonstrate their movements to each other.

NOTE: See Chapters 4 and 5 for a full description of activities, how they were modified and implemented for different age groups, the children's and teachers' reactions and reflections.

Teachers can modify and adapt all the activities to suit their particular needs. Also children will require varying degrees of support in the degree of scaffolding or structure that they need: obviously, younger children need to be supported more than older children; less able children need more support than more able children. However, it is important that the learners work using the TASC Problem-solving Wheel to guide their thinking and doing. The thinking can be shared through class discussion with the minimum of recording made in key words and in mindmap format on large sheets of paper so that they can be mounted in the classroom as prompts, and referred to in later discussions.

Appendix 1C

This appendix provides two checklists for reflection on preferred activities across the full range of human abilities.

CHECKLIST 1

Ways of thinking and learning (pupil checklist)

Everyone learns in a different way. Usually what we enjoy doing is how we learn best. Put a tick against each of the things you like doing. (*Tick as many boxes as you like.*) In each section, add up all of your ticks and write the total in the SCORE box. Your highest scores will tell you how you learn best.

1. THINGS I LIKE DOING – WORKING WITH OTHER PEOPLE

	✓		✓		✓		✓
Coaching sports and games		Working on a group project		Talking on the phone		Showing others how to do something	
Going to parties		Doing community work		Brainstorming ideas		Playing team sports	
Giving someone advice		Meeting other people		Doing drama and role play		Arguing my point of view	
						SCORE	

2. THINGS I LIKE DOING – WORKING ON MY OWN

	✓		✓		✓		✓
Solving problems		Having a hobby		Writing my diary		Being independent	
Being creative		Talking about my feelings		Reading and listening to music		Doing my own project	
Being in my own room		Making my own decisions		Making up my own mind		Studying on my own	
						SCORE	

3. THINGS I LIKE DOING – FINDING OUT ABOUT THE WORLD

	✓		✓		✓		✓
Going to church		Settling arguments		Reading ghost stories		Looking at the stars	
Being in a nature park		Watching films about space		Debating and arguing		Reading about time machines	
Reading about the past		Watching films like 'Lord of the Rings'		Going to a space museum		Finding out about things	
						SCORE	

4. THINGS I LIKE DOING – USING WORDS

Writing stories	✓	Making a speech	✓	Writing poems	✓	Telling jokes	✓
Talking		Telling a story		Reading magazines		Making up words	
Reading books		Learning a new language		Playing word games		Doing an interview	
						SCORE	

5. THINGS I LIKE DOING – MATHS ACTIVITIES

Drawing plans	✓	Doing number puzzles	✓	Playing card games	✓	Doing experiments	✓
Inventing things		Playing chess		Spotting the mistake		Going to museums	
Using a computer		Playing board games		Drawing diagrams		Giving directions	
						SCORE	

6. THINGS I LIKE DOING – SCIENTIFIC THINGS

Cooking a meal	✓	Watching Nature films	✓	Going on field trips	✓	Keeping a pet	✓
Doing experiments		Finding out how things work		Building and making things		Reading about science discoveries	
Finding things out for myself		Visiting or working on a farm		Visiting factories, exhibitions or museums		Exploring the countryside	
						SCORE	

7. THINGS I LIKE DOING – WORKING WITH MY HANDS

Making things	✓	Designing and drawing	✓	Playing with construction sets	✓	Playing computer games	✓
Building an electric train set		Playing chess and doing puzzles		Fixing and mending things		Using the computer to design things	
Working with machines		Using Lego and Multifix blocks		Making collages, sculptures and models		Taking things apart to see how they work	
						SCORE	

8. THINGS I LIKE DOING – USING PICTURES AND SHAPES

Doing jigsaws	✓	Visiting beautiful places	✓	Drawing cartoons	✓	Making sculptures	✓
Doing puzzles		Designing posters		Working on machines		Taking photos	
Putting up displays		Taking things to pieces		Decorating my room		Watching TV and videos	
						SCORE	

9. THINGS I LIKE DOING – THINGS WITH SOUND

	✓		✓		✓		✓
Singing songs		Whistling or humming		Background music		Unusual music	
Collecting CDs		Dancing		Relaxing to music		Going to concerts	
Using a synthesiser		Listening to classical music		Playing a musical instrument		Finding music for a play or a concert	
						SCORE	

10. THINGS I LIKE DOING – PHYSICAL THINGS

	✓		✓		✓		✓
Playing sport		Acting in a play		Doing pottery or craft		Gymnastics	
Going on field trips		Using tools and machines		Doing design and technology		Training for athletics	
Dancing		Doing judo or karate		Walking or swimming		Running or cycling	
						SCORE	

11. OTHER THINGS I ENJOY DOING

Write these down below.

DISCOVER TASC

CHECKLIST 2

Ways of thinking and learning: Multiple abilities (Teacher checklist)

We all have a mixture of each of the abilities, some more dominant than others.

Use the checklist below to reflect on your behaviour, dreams and the activities you enjoy. (*Tick if anything in the sentence applies to you.*) Score the 'oftens' in each section. Rank the sections in order.

Discuss whether this profile reflects your perceived range of your dominant abilities.

CHARACTERISTIC BEHAVIOUR	OFTEN	SOMETIMES	RARELY
1. SOCIAL/HUMANITARIAN ABILITY			
1. I am a natural leader, organiser, planner, chairperson.			
2. People ask me for advice, suggestions, ideas, help.			
3. I am 'streetwise', gregarious, enjoy socialising.			
4. I enjoy teaching, showing, demonstrating, guiding.			
5. I like to be involved in activities, team games, groups.			
6. I have a wide circle of friends, get on well with colleagues.			
7. I have good empathy, understanding, intuition, warmth.			
8. People choose my company, include/invite me out often.			
9. I am tolerant of faults and foibles, forgiving.			
10. I like talking, work well with others, enjoy crowds.			
2. EMOTIONAL ABILITY			
1. I am independent, strong-willed, a go-getter, a trend-setter.			
2. I have a realistic sense of my strengths and weaknesses.			
3. I work well on my own, am motivated, well-organised.			
4. I'm adaptable to living and learning styles.			
5. I'm self-contained, enjoy my own company, have a hobby.			
6. I can talk about my feelings, apologise, forgive and forget.			
7. I'm able to learn from personal success or failure.			
8. I feel good about myself, can ask for help.			
9. I'm even-tempered, can cope with other people.			
10. I can display affection, am very approachable, easy to get on with.			

CHARACTERISTIC BEHAVIOUR	OFTEN	SOMETIMES	RARELY
3. SPIRITUAL ABILITY			
1. I have strong intuition about people and situations.			
2. I am very concerned about current social issues.			
3. I belong to a voluntary association which cares for people.			
4. I am concerned about human rights and inequality.			
5. I enjoy discussions about the purpose of life.			
6. I think deeply about the 'big questions' in life.			
7. I'm very curious about how the world works.			
8. I value the qualities of compassion, love and caring for others			
9. I am reflective, self-observing and self-aware			
10. I am aware of the universe, feel part of humanity, close to nature.			
4. LINGUISTIC ABILITY			
1. I like writing and am better than average.			
2. I like talking, telling and listening to stories, jokes, rhymes, poems, puns.			
3. I like reading, word games, crosswords, quiz games.			
4. I'm good at spelling – I make intelligent approximations.			
5. I have a wide vocabulary. I enjoy writing letters, my diary.			
6. I'm a good verbal communicator. I can argue my point.			
7. I have wide general knowledge and a good memory.			
8. I speak coherently and confidently in public.			
9. I think in words rather than pictures or sensations.			
10. I enjoy word-processing, browsing on the Internet.			
5. LOGICAL/MATHEMATICAL ABILITY			
1. I ask a lot of questions: how, why, what, when, who?			
2. I like working with numbers, am good at calculations.			
3. I enjoy using a computer, particularly card games, puzzles.			
4. I enjoy strategy board games, brain teasers, problems.			
5. I enjoy classifying, making lists, putting things in order.			
6. I like to experiment, hypothesise, find mistakes.			
7. I like to analyse cause and effect, carry out 'What if...?' tasks.			
8. I like to find a way to make things work.			
9. I enjoy visits to museums, planetariums, exhibitions.			
10. I can write clear directions, instructions, plans.			

CHARACTERISTIC BEHAVIOUR	OFTEN	SOMETIMES	RARELY
6. SCIENTIFIC/REALISTIC ABILITY			
1. I'm interested in how things work. I like to experiment. I am systematic.			
2. I notice the fine detail in growth and seasons. I notice inconsistencies.			
3. I am interested in flora and fauna. I remember details of natural history.			
4. I am deeply concerned about issues concerning the environment.			
5. I have a good memory for scientific facts and principles.			
6. I enjoy solving problems. I am prepared to try different possible solutions.			
7. I like outdoor activities like sailing, fishing, walking, exploring new places.			
8. I am interested in astronomy, geography, biology, botany, physics, chemistry.			
9. I would like to have been a naturalist, an industrialist, a scientist, an explorer.			
10. I feel a close affinity with all wildlife. I appreciate the complexity of our world.			
7. MECHANICAL/TECHNICAL ABILITY			
1. I like working with tools, machines, engines, gadgets.			
2. I like manipulating computers and technology.			
3. I understand how things are assembled. I can repair things.			
4. I can work in 2D or 3D. I can adapt ideas.			
5. I can represent ideas visually, spatially, mathematically, verbally.			
6. I can apply ideas in new ways and contexts.			
7. I would like to have been an engineer, a designer, a mechanic.			
8. I enjoy 3D puzzles, chess, construction games and toys.			
9. I like to make things, I enjoy using my hands and my head.			
10. I like to experiment, take things apart, understand how things work.			
8. VISUAL/SPATIAL ABILITY			
1. I enjoy reading charts, maps, diagrams, pictures, displays.			
2. I have a tendency to daydream, have vivid night dreams.			
3. I enjoy art, craft, doodling, tinkering with machines.			
4. I enjoy visual images, tv, pictures, cartoons, videos.			
5. I like to build 3D structures, puzzles, 'do-it-yourself' jobs.			
6. I notice a gorgeous sky, a beautiful flower, a vivid display.			
7. I can recall exact shapes and sizes, patterns, colours.			
8. I like to study posters, charts, illustrations, graphics.			
9. I can read maps, can find my way around, I enjoy landscapes.			
10. I relax doing jigsaws, mazes, taking photographs, videos.			

CHARACTERISTIC BEHAVIOUR	OFTEN	SOMETIMES	RARELY
9. AUDITORY/SONAL ABILITY			
1. I always hear music in my head.			
2. I can tell when a note is off key, when a tune's not right.			
3. I can recall a song, a theme from a film, a signature tune.			
4. I can sing well, in tune, I listen to music a lot.			
5. I enjoy making music, I can pick out a tune easily.			
6. I have a rhythmic style of speaking, moving.			
7. I whistle, hum, sing to myself.			
8. I'm sensitive to noises, rain, wind, squeaks, whispers.			
9. Music influences my moods, feelings, reactions, nerves.			
10. I enjoy films, videos, concerts, dance.			
10. MOVEMENT/SOMATIC ABILITY			
1. I am well coordinated, enjoy sport, walking, cycling.			
2. I fidget, doodle, can copy mannerisms, gestures.			
3. I like to touch things, feel textures, shapes.			
4. I enjoy running, jumping, 'keep-fit', building, renovating.			
5. I have fine craft skills, cutting, sewing, constructing.			
6. I enjoy mime, drama, role play, dance, gymnastics.			
7. I learn best with 'hands-on', mechanical gadgets.			
8. I have 'gut instincts', am sensitive to body language.			
9. I wish I could have been a surgeon, engineer, sculptor.			
10. I get my best ideas jogging, doing the dishes, cleaning.			

Appendix 2

Appendix 2A

TASC: Thinking Actively in a Social Context
The TASC Problem-solving Wheel

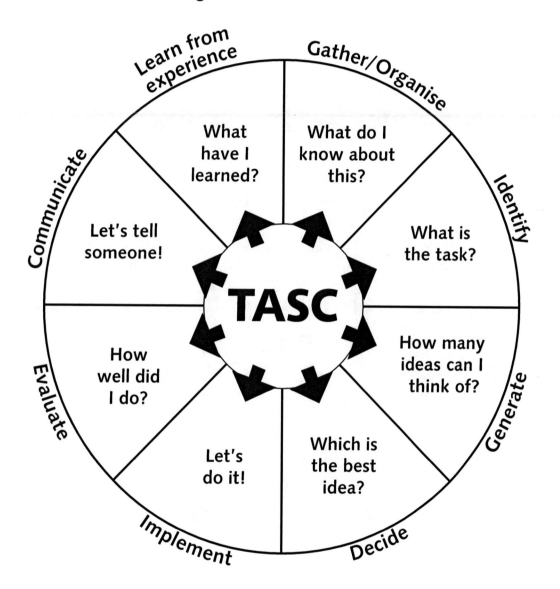

Children can cut and laminate the TASC Wheel and fasten it with paper-fasteners into an exercise book or thinking skills log-book. Better still, pupils can redesign the TASC Wheel and invent their own symbols for each stage of the Problem-solving Wheel. Then pupils can use the whole Wheel to guide their thinking and planning. It's a good idea to ask pupils to keep a portfolio of their best work which provides examples of the strategies they have used in developing their project. Importantly, the Problem-solving Process must be used across the curriculum whenever it is appropriate.

Appendix 2B

My Thinking and Planning Guide

Title of project: _____

Learn from experience

Gather/Organise

Communicate

Identify

What have I learned?

What do I know about this?

Let's tell someone!

My Project Plan

What is the task?

How well did I do?

How many ideas can I think of?

Evaluate

Generate

Let's do it!

Which is the best idea?

Implement

Decide

You can enlarge this activity sheet to A3 and pupils can use it to plan and record the stages of their thinking and problem-solving. It is a good idea for pupils to keep their activity record sheets in a thinking skills log-book or in a portfolio of their best work.

© Belle Wallace (2001) *Teaching Thinking Skills Across the Primary Curriculum*, David Fulton Publishers (in association with NACE).

Appendix 2C

TASC: Thinking Actively in a Social Context
The Core Tools for Effective Thinking

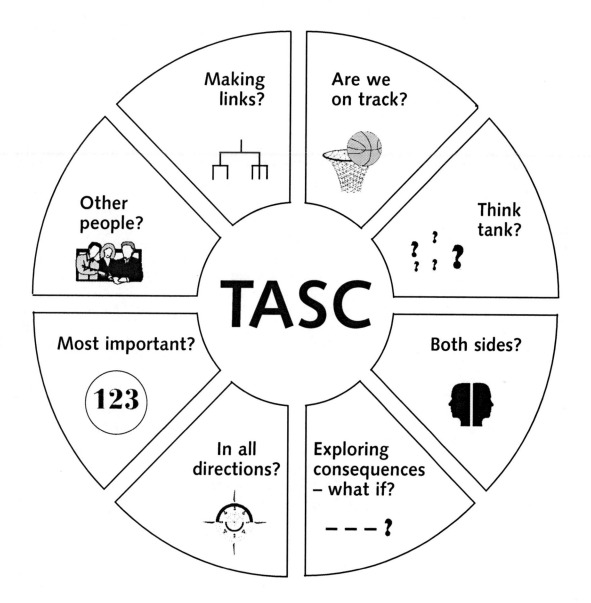

Appendix 2D

CHECKLIST 1

Teachers' assessment criteria for problem-solving abilities

Does the learner have? Is the learner able to?
Is there any evidence of?

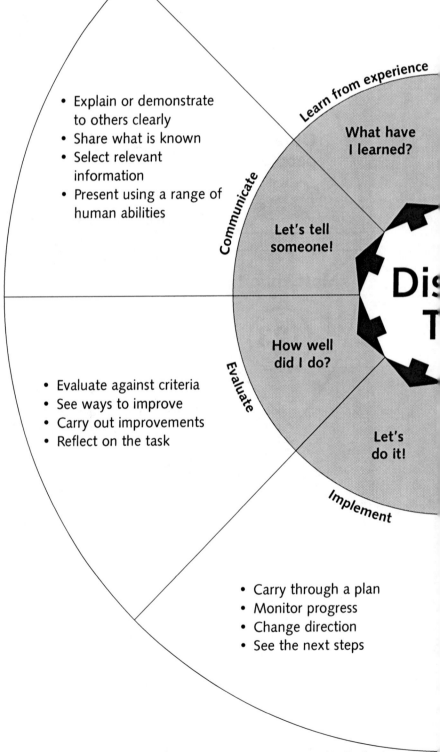

- Reflect on performance
- Transfer skills
- Retain new knowledge
- Articulate new skills

Learn from experience

What have I learned?

- Explain or demonstrate to others clearly
- Share what is known
- Select relevant information
- Present using a range of human abilities

Communicate

Let's tell someone!

Dis
T

How well did I do?

Evaluate

- Evaluate against criteria
- See ways to improve
- Carry out improvements
- Reflect on the task

Let's do it!

Implement

- Carry through a plan
- Monitor progress
- Change direction
- See the next steps

- Wide knowledge of topic
- Recall of extended information
- Sound understanding of advanced concepts
- Ability to organise data in complex groups

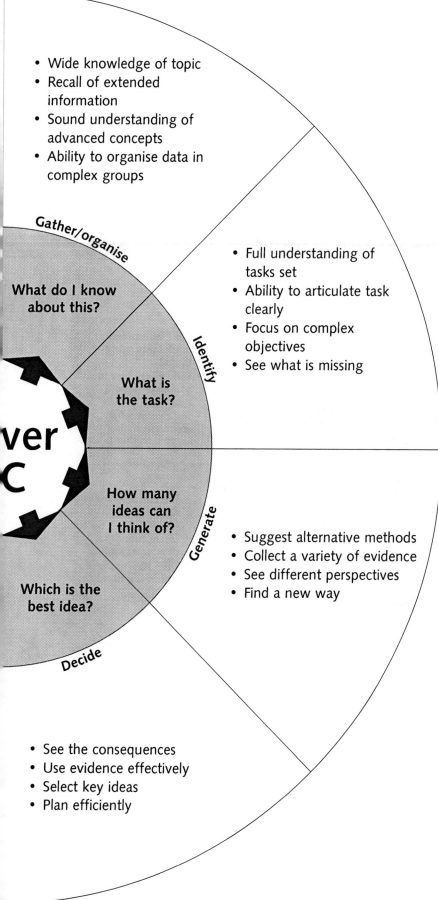

Gather/organise

What do I know about this?

- Full understanding of tasks set
- Ability to articulate task clearly
- Focus on complex objectives
- See what is missing

Identify

What is the task?

How many ideas can I think of?

Generate

- Suggest alternative methods
- Collect a variety of evidence
- See different perspectives
- Find a new way

Which is the best idea?

Decide

- See the consequences
- Use evidence effectively
- Select key ideas
- Plan efficiently

CHECKLIST 2

Assessing my project

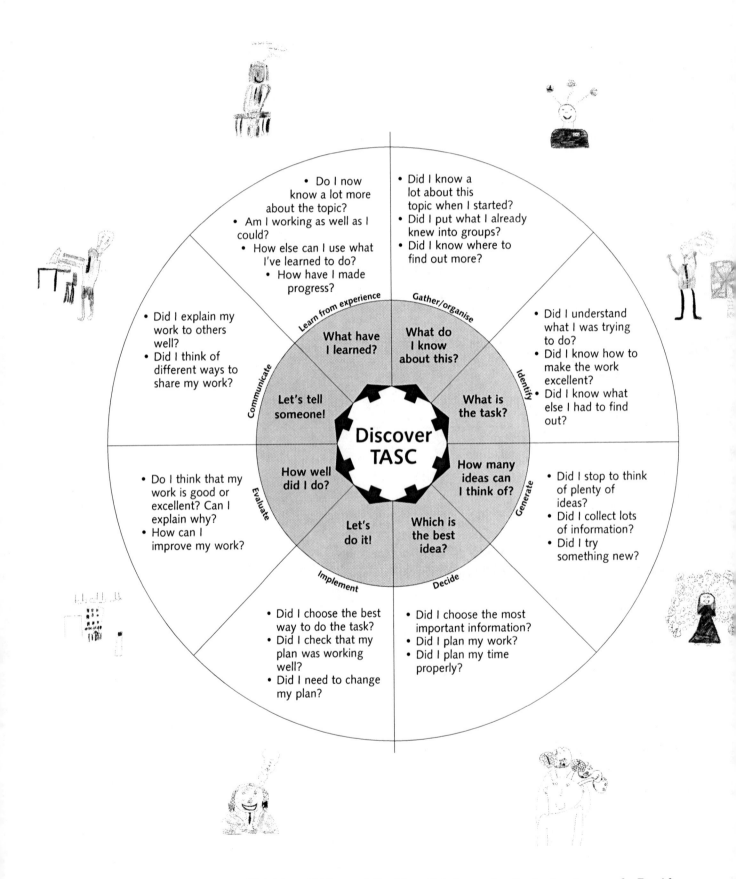

DISCOVER TASC

Appendix 3

Appendix 3A

Analysis of problem types for lesson planning

Type 1 problem	Type 2 problem	Type 3 problem	Type 4 problem	Type 5 problem	Type 6 problem
1a. Meet specific goal 1b. Well-defined purposes 2. Use/Practise new/known technique 3. Correct answer/solution	1a. Meet specific goal 1b. Well-defined purposes 2a. Choose right/best method 2b. Decide/Apply right/best method 3. Correct answer/solution	1a. Meet specific goal 1b. Well-defined purposes 2a. Create/Generate new ways 2b. Use varied ways 3. Correct answer/solution	1a. Meet specific goal 1b. Well-defined purposes 2a. Create/Generate own ways (Use specified criteria) 2b. Choose best method 3. Choose best answer/solution (Use specified criteria)	1a. Meet specific goal 1b. Well-defined purposes 2a. Create/Generate own ways (Use own criteria) 2b. Choose best method 3. Choose best answer/solution (Use own criteria)	1a. Decide on own problem/challenge 1b. Define own problem/challenge 1c. Meet personally identified goal/challenge 2a. Create/Generate own ways (Use own criteria) 2b. Choose best method 3. Choose best answer/solution (Use own criteria)

Note: The differences between Type 1 problem (closed) and Type 6 problem (open) are clear and it is easy to differentiate between the two types. Problem Types 2, 3, 4 and 5 form more of a continuum with blurred edges, and often it is in the *wording* of the problem that the problem *type* becomes clear.

See the wording of the examples of problem types in the lesson planning in Chapter 4 (pp. 81–4) for clear practical examples of the problem types.

© June Maker (2004) *Thinking Skills and Problem-Solving – An Inclusive Approach,* David Fulton Publishers.

Appendix 3B

I can analyse the types of problems I have solved

When you have completed a topic of work, you can think about the types of problems you have been solving. If you want to keep some examples of problems, photocopy your work and label it with the problem type.

Problem Type	My observations	Agree ✓
TYPE 1 I was given a problem that needed to be solved OR I knew the problem that needed to be solved	● There was *one way to solve it* ● There was *one right answer*	
TYPE 2 I was given a problem that needed to be solved OR I knew the problem that needed to be solved	● There were *several ways to solve it* ● There was *one right answer*	
TYPE 3 I was given a problem that needed to be solved OR I knew the problem that needed to be solved	● I thought of *new ways to solve it* ● There was *one right answer*	
TYPE 4 I was given a problem that needed to be solved OR I knew the problem that needed to be solved	● I thought of *new ways to solve it* ● There was *more than one answer* ● I *chose the best answer*	
TYPE 5 I *decided* on the problem I needed to solve	● I found *new ways to solve it* ● There was *more than one answer* ● I *chose the best answer*	
TYPE 6 I *found* the problem I wanted to solve	● I found *new ways to solve it* ● I *decided whether my solution was successful*	

Appendix 3C

A menu of activities across the multiple abilities

Linguistic/Verbal	Mathematical
essays, stories, poems, letters, diaries, crosswords, word puzzles, quiz games, debates, speeches, research, audio-tapes, video programmes, PowerPoint, interviews, newspapers, magazines, Internet, reports, questionnaires	questionnaires, puzzles, graphs, charts, diagrams, inventing, games, flowcharts, mindmaps, timelines, Venn diagrams, plans, maps, collections, museums, designs, inventions, PowerPoint
Visual/Spatial	**Movement**
charts, maps, diagrams, pictures, displays, sketches, constructions, television, videos, films, cartoons, comic strips, adverts, pictures, puzzles, photographs, posters, illustrations, jigsaws, mazes, sculptures, murals, collages, PowerPoint, spreadsheets	drama, puppetry, role play, dance, constructions, design technology, craft, interviews, field trips, sketching, games, re-enactments, modelling, sculptures, rap
Musical/Auditory	**Social**
songs, rap, drama, dance, compositions, audio-tapes, video, programmes, radio, concerts, performances, plays	debates, discussions, brainstorming, group work, demonstrations, emailing, bulletin boards, interviews, drama, role play, puppetry, dance, speeches
Emotional/Personal	**Spiritual**
projects, research, hobbies, collections, newspapers, magazines, radio, videos, diaries, speeches, poems, stories, puzzles, letters	debates, poems, displays, adverts, community projects, videos, essays, exhibitions, questionnaires, interviews, surveys, role play
Scientific	**Mechanical/Technical**
field trips, collections, nature walks, a wild area, experiments, sketches, exhibitions, photographs, investigations, projects, displays, videos, research, inventions, constructions	constructions, machines, PowerPoint, designs, sketches, building, making, computers, design technology, craft, modelling

Note: Each activity encompasses more than one ability, but the activity has been placed within the dominant ability.

References and Further Reading

Adams, H. B. (1985) 'The teaching of general problem solving strategies', in *Developing Cognitive Strategies in Young Children*, SAALED Conference Proceedings, October 1985, University of Durban-Westville, South Africa.

Adams, H. B. (1986) 'Teaching general problem solving strategies in the classroom', *Gifted Education International*, 4(2), pp. 84–9.

Bandura, A. (1971) *Social Learning Theory*. Englewood Cliffs, NJ: Prentice Hall.

Bandura, A. (1982) 'Self-efficacy mechanism in human agency', *American Psychologist*, 37, pp. 122–47.

Black, P. and Wiliam, D. (1998) *Inside the Black Box: Raising Standards through Classroom Assessment*. London: King's College London.

Black, P., Harrison, C., Lee, C., Marshall, B. and Wiliam, D. (2004) *Working Inside the Black Box: Assessment for Learning in the Classroom*. London: Nfer-Nelson.

Borkowski, J. E. (1985) 'Signs of intelligence: strategy generalization and metacognition', in R. S. Yussen (ed.) *The Growth of Reflective Thought in Children*. New York: Academic Press.

Brown, A. L. (1987) 'Metacognition, executive control, self regulation and other more mysterious mechanisms', in F. E. Weinert and R. H. Kluwe (eds) *Metacognition, Motivation and Understanding*. Hillsdale, NJ: Lawrence Erlbaum.

Brown, A. L. and Campione, J. C. (1994) 'Guided discovery in a community of learners', in K. McGilly (ed.) *Classroom Lessons: Integrating cognitive theory and classroom practice*. Cambridge, MA: MIT Press.

Brown, A. L. and Ferrara, R. A. (1985) 'Diagnosing zones of proximal development', in J. V. Wertsch (ed.) *Culture, Communication and Cognition: Vygotskian Perspectives*. New York: Cambridge University Press.

Bruner, J. (1985) 'Vygotsky: A historical and conceptual perspective', in J. V. Wertsch (ed.) *Culture, Communication and Cognition: Vygotskian Perspectives*. New York: Cambridge University Press.

Chipman, S. F., Segal, J. W. and Glaser, R. (eds) (1985) *Thinking and Learning Skills Vol. 2: Research and Open Questions*. Hillsdale, NJ: Lawrence Erlbaum.

Cole, M. (1985) 'The zone of proximal development: Where culture and cognition create each other', in J. V. Wertsch (ed.) *Culture, Communication and Cognition: Vygotskian Perspective*. New York: Cambridge University Press.

Cole, M., Gay, J., Glick, J. and Sharp, D. W. (1971) *The Cultural Context of Learning and Thinking*. New York: Basic Books.

Damasio, A. (1999) *The Feeling of What Happens: Body, emotion and the making of consciousness.* London: Heinemann.

Feuerstein, R. and Shalom, H. (1986) 'The learning potential assessment device', in B. W. Richards (ed.) *Proceedings of the First Congress of the International Association for the Scientific Study of Mental Deficiency.* Reigate, UK: Michael Jackson.

Flavell, J. H. (1979) 'Metacognition and cognitive monitoring: A new area of cognitive-development enquiry', *American Psychologist*, **34**, pp. 906–1011.

Flavell, J. H. (1985) *Cognitive Development* (2nd edn). Englewood Cliffs, NJ: Prentice Hall.

Foreman, E. A. and Cazden, C. B. (1985) 'Exploring Vygotskian perspectives in education', in J. V. Wertsch (ed.) *Culture, Communication and Cognition: Vygotskian Perspectives.* New York: Cambridge University Press.

Gardner, H. (1983) *Frames of Mind: The Theory of Multiple Intelligences.* New York: Basic Books.

Gardner, H. (1999) *Intelligences Reframed: Multiple Intelligences for the 21st Century.* New York: Basic Books.

Getzels, J. W. and Csikszentmihalyi, M. (1967) 'Scientific creativity', *Science Journal,* **3**(9), pp. 80–4.

Getzels, J. W. and Csikszentmihalyi, M. (1976) *The Creative Vision: A Longitudinal Study of Problem Finding in Art.* New York: Wiley Books.

Goleman, D. (1996) *Emotional Intelligence.* London: Bloomsbury.

Leyden, S. (2002) *Supporting the Child of Exceptional Ability at Home and at School* (3rd edn). London: David Fulton Publishers, in association with NACE.

Maker, C. J. (2001) 'DISCOVER: Assessing and developing problem-solving'. *Gifted Education International*, **15**(3), pp. 232–51.

Maker, C. J. and Anuruthwong, U. (in press) <details to come from Belle in proofs>

Maker, C. J. and King, M. (1996) *Nurturing Giftedness in Young Children.* Reston, VA: The Council for Exceptional Children (www.cec.sped.org).

Maker, C. J. and Schiever, S. (in press) *Teaching Models in Education of the Gifted* (3rd edn). Austin, TX: Pro-Ed.

Porter, L. (1999) *Gifted Young Children: A Guide for Teachers and Parents.* Buckingham: Open University Press.

Salovey, P. and Mayer, J. D. (1990) 'Emotional intelligence', *Imagination, Cognition and Personality*, **9**, pp. 185–211.

Schiever, S. and Maker, J. (1997) 'Enrichment and Acceleration: An overview and new directions', in G. Davis and N. Colangelo (eds), *Handbook of Gifted Education* (2nd edn). Needham Heights, MA: Allyn & Bacon, pp. 113–25.

Segal, J. W., Chipman, S. F. and Glaser, R. (eds) (1985) *Thinking and Learning Skills Vol. 1: Relating Instruction to Research.* Englewood Cliffs, NJ: Lawrence Erlbaum.

Sternberg, R. J. (1983) 'Criteria for intelligence skills training', *Educational Researcher*, **12**, pp. 6–12.

Sternberg, R. J. (1985) *Beyond IQ: A Triarchic Theory of Human Intelligence.* New York: Cambridge University Press.

Sternberg, R. J. (1986) *Intelligence Applied: Understanding and Increasing your Intellectual Skills.* New York: Harcourt Brace Jovanovich.

Sternberg, R. J. (1996) *Cognitive Psychology.* New York: Harcourt Brace College Publishers.

Vygotsky, L. S. (1978) *Mind in Society. The Development of Higher Psychological Processes* (edited and translated by W. Cole *et al.*). Cambridge, MA: Harvard University Press.

Wallace, B. (2000) *Teaching the Very Able Child: Developing a Policy for Adopting Strategies for Provision.* London: David Fulton Publishers, in association with NACE.

Wallace, B. (ed.) (2001) *Teaching Thinking Skills Across the Primary Curriculum: A practical approach for all abilities.* London: David Fulton Publishers, in association with NACE.

Wallace, B. (ed.) (2002) *Teaching Thinking Skills Across the Early Years: A practical approach for children aged 4–7.* London: David Fulton Publishers, in association with NACE.

Wallace, B. (2003a) *Using History to Develop Thinking Skills at Key Stage 2.* London: David Fulton Publishers, in association with NACE.

Wallace, B. (2003b) *Assessment Strategies for More Able Children.* London: Qualifications and Curriculum Authority/Department of Education and Skills.

Wallace, B. and Adams, H. B. (1993a) *TASC Thinking Actively in a Social Context.* Oxford: AB Academic Publishers.

Wallace, B. and Adams, H. B. (eds) (1993b) *Worldwide Perspectives on the Gifted Disadvantaged.* Oxford: AB Academic Publishers.

Wallace, B. and Bentley, R. (eds) (2002) *Teaching Thinking Skills Across the Middle Years: A practical approach for children aged 9–17.* London: David Fulton Publishers, in association with NACE.

Wertsch, J. V. (1985) 'Introduction', in J. V. Wertsch (ed.) *Culture, Communication and Cognition: Vygotskian Perspectives.* New York: Cambridge University Press.

Wertsch, J. V. (1985) 'Adult–child interactions as a source of self-regulation in children', in S. R. Yussen (ed.) *The Growth of Reflective Thinking in Children.* New York: Academic Press.

Wertsch, J. V. and Addison Stone, C. (1985) 'The concept of internalization in Vygotsky's account of the genesis of higher mental functions', in J. V. Wertsch (ed.) *Culture, Communication and Cognition: Vygotskian Perspectives.* New York: Cambridge University Press.

Wiliam, D. and Black, P. (1999) *Assessment and Classroom Learning.* London: King's College London.

Websites

National Association for Able Children in Education (NACE)
www.nace.co.uk (see for TASC website)
www.discover.arizona.edu

Index

Lightning Source UK Ltd.
Milton Keynes UK
UKOW02f2126120813

215264UK00012B/333/A